Automatic Exit:
Turn Your Service Business into a Sellable Asset

Copyright © 2024 Shawn Butler and Relevant Publishing. All rights reserved.

ISBN: 9798346084259

Cataloging-in-Publication data is available.

No part of this publication may be reproduced, distributed, or transmitted in any form or by any means, including photocopying, recording, or electronic or mechanical methods, without the prior written permission of the author and publisher, except in the case of brief quotations embodied in critical reviews and certain other noncommercial uses permitted by copyright law.

Disclaimer: The author makes no guarantees concerning the level of success you may experience by following the advice and strategies contained in this book, and you accept the risk that results will differ for each individual. The testimonials and examples provided in this book show exceptional results, which may not apply to the average reader and are not intended to represent or guarantee that you will achieve the same or similar results.

Automatic Exit:
Turn Your Service Business into a Sellable Asset

By Shawn Butler

Dedication

If I were going to write a book for me, I would write about spaceships or magic.

Or both.

But I wrote this book for you, the business owner that wants to become a business seller.

It's about your life and *your life's work*—how you can take what you've built, what got you where you are, and turn it into the launchpad that rockets you to where you want to be next and, like alchemy, transforms your business into something new and amazing, wonderful, and even magical.

So, in a way, this actually *is* a book about spaceships and magic.

-Shawn

Table of Contents

Introduction

PART 1 – Running a Service Business

    Chapter 1: The Unsolvable Problem

    Chapter 2: Start Where You Are

    Chapter 3: Why You Should Sell Your Business

    Chapter 4: The Role of Value Creation

PART 2 – The Automatic Exit Framework

    Step 1: Decide Who You Serve

    Step 2: Solve the Biggest Problem

    Step 3: Be the Best in the World

    Step 4: Make It McDonald's

    Step 5: Assign Seats

    Step 6: Line Them Up Like Coke Bottles

    Step 7: Fire Your Clients

    Step 8: Fire Yourself

    Step 9: Set Fire to Everything

    Step 10: Now, Cross the Bridge

PART 3 – Becoming a Business Seller

    Chapter 5: Implementing the Automatic Exit

    Chapter 6: My Story and Your Story

Conclusion

Introduction

I have seen so many books about how to become an entrepreneur, how to build a business, and even how to buy or sell a business, but I haven't found one yet that bridges the gap from how to go from being an "owner" of a small service business engaged in the running, growing, and managing of that business to being a "seller" of a small business—making the crucial shift from seeing everything you've built from the inside to taking an outsider point of view that lets you see the true value of what you've created.

Not to mention a book on how to *become* that person—the one who has successfully *sold* (notice the use of the past-tense) that service business and lived to tell about it.

For me, business ownership has always been a lesson in self-definition. We are different things at different times—entrepreneur, inventor, manager, technician (hat tip Michael E. Gerber)—but I urge you to start now to think of yourself not as a business owner: "someone who started a business," or even "a person running a business," but going forward, redefine yourself as "someone who is preparing a business to sell."

Let that sink in.

You are now in a different phase of your business. You must become someone who is preparing your business to sell. You should feel different already, actually, and that's normal. Because an important distinction happens for all business owners when they make the recognition that *they are not the business.* The business was never you, and you were never defined by the business you own.

The business is altogether a separate thing. A thing that you do, like a hobby or sport. Your occupation and avocation never would define you. Not entirely. An actor, adventurer, animator, archer, artist, athlete, or author is still a person that *does* those things, not someone entirely defined by them (and that's just starting with the "A's"). An actor acts, an animator animates, an author authors things... or writes. Okay, that one is irregular.

So, a business owner owns? For too many business owners, we define ourselves by our ownership of the business. I call it keeping the "own" in ownership by insisting that it is your *own* business. As soon as it's bigger than you, it's no longer about you. Don't fight to keep the "own" in ownership.

As with the list of jobs above, the key is in the verb we pair with the noun. An owner *owns*—the person who owns a business is too close to it, too personally tied up in it, or worse, too buried in the business to see it objectively.

Speaking of being buried, the origin of the French word for entrepreneur, *entreprendre*, literally means "to undertake," as in you are "the undertaker" for the business you want to build. Think about that the next time you say, "This job is killing me."

But a seller *sells.* That's where we need to be.

Robert Kiyosaki, author of *Rich Dad, Poor Dad*, once illustrated this difference when he was criticized for the level of writing in his bestselling book. Kiyosaki reportedly replied to the interviewer that he was a best*selling* author, not a best*writing* author.

He saw the difference clearly. A writer *writes.* A seller *sells.* The business owner *owns* the business, but those business owners *preparing* their business to sell now spend their time as "the seller" principally on activities that will set the business up to sell, that will benefit the eventual buyer, and add value to the ultimate deal.

This book will walk you through what those activities should be, how to do them, and the best order to approach them. It will help you become a "business seller" on the path to eventually being someone who *has sold* the business you built.

See the use of the past tense? That's powerful.

"Someone who has sold a business" is the person you want to become next. Don't lose sight of that.

Selling a business is not a simple process, but it starts with a rather simple decision to change your perspective. And that change of perspective changes all the other pieces.

This book is the accumulation of my own personal experience building and selling three businesses combined with my experience consulting hundreds of other service business owners where I have retold this same story you're about to read and retaught this same simple but powerful lesson:

Your business is worth more than you think.

You have invested your time and energy, your sweat, even your tears, and, in the largest sense, some of the best hours, days, and even years of your life into building and running your business.

And now I have the unique privilege of telling you what I have told so many others before you—that your investment was not a futile exchange of so many hours for dollars and services rendered, but was, in fact, an overarching success story of building an important and significant asset that will have a great value to those people who are in a position to appreciate it.

Like a goldminer digging his tunnel to and from the goldmine, in building your business, you have built the path to your own source of wealth now and into the future.

Yes, this story is about me, my past businesses and my past clients, but it is about you and the future of your business.

I want to share this story as directly as possible to be sure I communicate to each business owner that reads it that you have created a thing of value. By understanding that, you can begin today to capture that value, to increase its value to the eventual buyer, and to enact a plan that will lead to a satisfying ending to the story of your business.

Let's begin that story. The story about me and my past business that is really a story about you and your future.

Automatic Exit:
Turn Your Service Business into a Sellable Asset

PART 1 – Running a Service Business

Chapter 1: The Unsolvable Problem

My business was nearly four years old when we suddenly faced the unsolvable problem.

We both know that young businesses face hundreds of problems every day—sometimes even at night—so, having a new problem, even a big problem, wasn't news to any of us.

But this was the most serious problem we had yet encountered, and to be honest, it was beyond anything we'd imagined or prepared for.

This was not just a really big problem, this was THE problem. And there is no solution to it.

You see, since the beginning of our business, we had never had a product to sell to our customers. We had gained customers, charged them money, collected the money, and done the work, but we had never delivered a single product into their hands. And we were now four years old and billing over two hundred thousand dollars a month.

Were we a scam?

Technically, we were a "lead generation" business, a company in the business of providing our clients with new leads from qualified prospects that they could nurture to eventually generate their own new clients. It was an important business, and we provided a valuable service for our clients.

But what did we actually sell?

We sold our clients a list of services that we knew their business needed. They picked the services, we did the work and delivered the results, but we didn't actually sell "leads." What we sold was more accurately described as "lead generation activities"—the hours and the expertise that went into delivering the result they wanted.

What we actually sold was a service.

And that was at the core of the unsolvable problem we now faced. We didn't have a product to sell, we were selling time and expertise and results. So how can we sell a product if the product itself doesn't exist?

What Does Your Business Sell?

Let me pause here to address the elephant in our story—if you're like me and my business, you run your own service business. You provide a solution or solve a problem for your clients in exchange for money. That's business, right?

But service businesses are unique because we don't fit the strictest definition of what makes a business a "business" – we don't *make* anything.

In my first semester of business school, they taught that the ideal of business was to provide a manufactured good, famously termed a "widget" by university professors, and to sell that widget to many, many paying customers. Furthermore, the definition of a *successful* business is to produce a widget for x and sells that widget for $x + y$ where x is the cost of the good and y is that critical factor of business ownership: profit!

Does all of that sound right to you? Good. That means we've all read the same business books!

With that definition clear in our minds, the goal for a successful business is to reduce the cost x to produce the widget as efficiently as possible and increase the price $x + y$ of the widget to create the greatest possible profit.

But here's the problem—if you're running a service business, you have no widget!

Owners of service businesses have no manufacturing, no inventory, no retail channels or store fronts, and no cost of goods sold that we can decrease in order to increase profits.

We just have people providing our customers with a service.

People are Not Widgets

Don't get me wrong, we both know that service businesses have huge advantages when compared to manufacturing and retail:

1. Low (or no) overhead
2. No shelving requirements
3. No inventory or product turnover issues
4. The factories don't breakdown
5. The equipment doesn't need repairs
6. Inventory is never delayed by breakdowns in supply chain

But we have one huge disadvantage—everything we sell relies on our people. And to overstate the obvious, people are not widgets.

For almost four years our service business had been the outgrowth of our original four-person team. Each person was responsible for his own area of expertise regarding what our clients needed and how to deliver that result.

The "widget" that we sold was the result of our expertise combined with our hours of individual work. This is how most service businesses work.

And, unfortunately, it's also the definition of a business *that cannot scale!*

The business had grown to more than 20 employees servicing some 80-odd clients and the four partners each headed an individual department over one aspect of the business.

Division of Labor

The title and assignment will vary from business to business, but the general roles are the same for all companies: selling, billing, and delivering.

For us, the CEO was in charge of determining our services, the VP of Marketing was in charge of selling our services, the COO of fulfilling our services, and the VP of Technology in charge of supporting our services through tools, tech, and automation. It was a precariously balanced system of mutual interdependence, but it worked.

At least it *had* worked until we were presented with our biggest and most unsolvable problem.

One of our people was leaving. Our COO had been accepted to grad school and would be gone in nine months.

The unsolvable problem we found in our business, and that I've since uncovered with every one of my clients' businesses, is that a service business relies on people.

And people are inherently unreliable.

Fixing the Unsolvable Problem

With this announcement from one of our key people, we suddenly found ourselves facing the single biggest problem we had been able to ignore for the past several years—the fact that we were a business entirely dependent on people!

With his departure, we knew we would have to rethink our business and find new ways to provide our services for our clients, because when he left, he would take with him all of the thinking, ideas, and undocumented processes that had been supporting his area of the business.

Can you see why this was a big problem? Does your business have this problem?

I first called this problem "unsolvable" because most problems in business actually are solved the same way: you throw money at it.

With a little money (or a lot), it's easy to buy a new tool, switch to a new vendor or service provider, or simply hire a new person who can step in and do that job. But with the departure of one of the founders, we suddenly saw all of the fragile flaws that were lurking beneath the surface of our business.

This change revealed our business was a house of cards. We had built up and up into a multi-story building without ever looking down to see that we'd begun our construction on a foundation of sand. And now it was all in danger of being washed away.

But in a way, we had been given a gift.

Rebuilding our House of Cards

We now were able to clearly see what the problem was and had been given a clear timeline to fix it. We knew we had just less than a year before our COO left to figure out our solution, so we would put emergency scaffolding in place, and rebuild.

Like rebuilding after the Great Fire of Paris, we used the crisis as a new chance to lay out a better plan with a more stable and long-term foundation.

Now I'll jump ahead in this story and tell you how it ended. Don't worry, we'll come right back here and fill in all the gaps we're skipping over! But at this point in our fairytale story, it's important you know that we all lived happily ever after.

Well, happily enough.

After just 5 years in business, we received a mid-seven figure valuation and sold our company to a competitor that—putting it bluntly—got much more than they paid for, but, at the same time, didn't truly appreciate the value of the business they'd acquired.

By the way, I've since had it verified that this is the most typical result of all company exits. **In fact, over 75% of business owners who have sold their business experience regret within a year after the sale, according to reports from the Exit Planning Institute.**

And you'll be relieved to know that our four intrepid young entrepreneurs have since gone on to find new life paths to pursue and new measurements for success and a life of fulfillment.

The Lessons We Learned

For me, personally, in the intervening years, I've been able to look back and recognize that, given the chance to do this again, we should have taken much longer, built the value much larger, set up our systems and services much more thoughtfully, and sold the company more intentionally ... as well as for a lot more money!

Again, I've found that this is also typical of the business exit experience.

And I shared the ending first because, to really unpack and appreciate the many lessons of my story, I need you to know how it turned out. We were fine. Things worked out. It all ends well.

But we didn't know that back when we were where you are now.

That's still back at the point when things felt scary, uncertain, even overwhelming, and sometimes out of our control. That's the hard part, the part you're most likely in now. And, unfortunately, it will get harder. At this stage, I have to warn you that things get worse before they get better.

So, let me take you back to the beginning of our little service company and tell you how we got from where we were: scared, uncertain, and overwhelmed, to a successful exit, and finding confident new beginnings for all of us—and share how that experience has shaped the consulting and advisement I've given to hundreds of business owners since then to help them understand the actual value of the businesses they've built and establish a plan—starting immediately!—to get the greatest return on their valuable asset.

If you've read this far, I'm pausing here to tell you I appreciate you. This paragraph is an *Easter Egg!* to reward you for actually reading the book. We'll get right back to the story, but, you see, I'm a reader... but I get that not everybody is.

Reading takes effort and commitment, as well as a dedication of time. Those ideals are becoming less popular.

As a writer and academic, I have a great respect for the discipline required to codify thought into written word. But as an entrepreneur and business owner, I also have great respect for time and I value succinctness as well as clearly conveying the most valuable message.

If you continue reading, you'll notice I've included many precious gold nuggets of advice and gems of hard-earned wisdom that will be worth your time and effort to uncover and implement. This type of reading has its own reward. However, to prove the value of this book right up front for my impatient audience of "ready, fire, aim" entrepreneurs and empire builders, the TL;DR* summary of what comes next is spelled out here:

---

*TL;DR - Abbreviation for "too long; didn't read" developed as internet slang to indicate that the person posting either didn't read the text in its entirety (if at all) or to introduce a summary of a longer section of text. I'm including this here simply because I find it funny that the footnote to explain the acronym is longer than simply explaining the concept in the text itself. #efficiency

The Automatic Exit Framework:
How to Turn Your Service Business into a Sellable Asset

1. Decide who you serve.
2. Solve the biggest problem.
3. Be the best in the world.
4. Make it McDonald's.
5. Assign Seats.
6. Line them up like Coke bottles.
7. Fire your clients.
8. Fire yourself.
9. Set fire to everything.
10. Now, cross the bridge.

There you go! That is the bullet point version of the lessons I learned from growing, scaling, and selling my own service-based business as well as the process and method I advise for my clients. This certainly does not tell you everything I learned or give you enough to do this for your own business, but that's what the rest of this book is designed to do.

As you finish the first chapter, I want to reward you right up front by doing what every good writer should do: deliver on the promise of the story.

Famed author and story doctor, David Farland, taught that the storyteller's job at the outset is to establish the promise of the story, then proceed to fulfill that promise through the rest of the story, and ultimately over-deliver against the audience's expectations.

If the story were about rescuing an ancient relic, like in George Lucas' *Indiana Jones and the Raiders of the Lost Ark*, the promise would be that there will be action, danger, and exciting adventures in exotic locations. The storyteller delivers on that promise in the very first scene by presenting his hero risking his life to outfight, or at least outsmart, bad guys and outwit tripwires and traps amid ancient ruins.

That is the method for telling a great story, just as the list above is the method for creating a valuable, sellable business. But the art is not in simply knowing the method, but in the actual performance of it. Not just knowing the story, but in the actual telling of the story.

Now, let's get back to the story.

Chapter 2 – Start Where You Are

For me, thirty-five was the perfect age to become an entrepreneur.

I was old enough to finally feel like I knew some things, but young enough not to realize how much I still had to learn.

By this age I'd worked ten-plus years in the advertising industry, investing my time into helping grow other people's ad agencies, until I finally arrived at the point where I felt ready to do it for myself.

In some ways, I was simply transitioning what I'd been doing for bosses and clients over to making money for myself using the same skills I'd already developed.

In other ways, it was the hardest thing I'd ever faced, requiring completely new skills, and I had no idea what I was getting myself into! Knowing none of that in advance, I stepped off the proverbial cliff and began running my own small marketing agency along with three partners who complimented and balanced my interests and skill set.

And it changed the trail and trajectory of my life.

Determining Your Trail Markers

Like all new businesses, we started fresh, signing up a few clients, and eagerly setting off down the trail, knowing we would have to simply figure many things out as we went. But there were, for us, a few key points that guided our direction and momentum right out of the gate.

Your business has these key points, too. We call them Trail Markers because they mark the point where you set off from the well-traveled road and departed down your business's own untraveled path.

The Trail Markers are the aspects of the business that are initially shaped by your individual background along with that of your partners or senior team members. Trail Markers come from your initial clients and the initial services you provide. And they come naturally, shaped by the location of your business, your clients, vendors, and even your employees.

Questions to uncover potential Trail Markers:

1. What did you do before starting the business that guided the direction of the business?
2. What influence did the background of your people make on the business?
3. How about your geography?
4. Your choice of clients?
5. The industry or specialization of your service?

Take a moment to examine these often-subtle influences that carried weight on the direction you initially took with your business.

Knowing what your Trail Markers were when the company started out will help you identify the place where you started from, and the origin of many of the key assumptions, common traits, and habits—good and bad—that show up later in your company culture.

Here's how that played out for us:

In my personal background, along with a decade of ad agency experience, I also had spent seven years in academia, earning two master's degrees, including an MBA, and teaching as an adjunct professor and guest lecturer at several colleges and universities. I loved marketing and the psychology behind buying and selling, and, like my dad, I was a natural storyteller and teacher, so I always sought chances to teach others the things I was learning in my work.

With that Trail Marker, it makes sense that we set up our business on the edge of campus between two of the universities where I taught. The other founders were also college grads and natural teachers, so it also may not surprise you that we invested considerable effort into building and maintaining a relationship with the professors and academic advisors at those schools and setup an approved internship for students in the marketing, business, and communications programs there.

Academic Learning Meets Business Practice

I'll share more on this later, but it's important to note that during those first years in business, our internship program proved invaluable in providing two things our business needed:

Number one, we gained access to smart, ambitious workers from both the free and paid interns that we brought in and trained. And here it's important to note that we didn't have them printing copies or running for coffees. We created a top-tier internship program that gave students real-world experience in performing client work.

This gave them a taste of the actual work of a marketing agency, throwing them right in on real tasks for our actual clients so they could test whether they were good at it, or if they even liked this business. For us, this led to really productive team members, deep talent on the bench, and a strong academic-minded culture around the office.

It also gave us *really* low-cost work outputs—but more on that later!

And in turn, we gave the employees that came through our internship marketable skills and real-world credentials to hit the ground running at graduation, and many of them went on to make a difference and be a great benefit in the industry.

This was fulfilling for us as owners. Even though sometimes it meant training someone great only to see them go to work for a competitor, we recognize that every individual has to seek his or her own path. It is part of the risk you take as a business owner, and honestly, as a human being, when you invest in another person—be it time, money, or just your concern for that person and their life choices—and have it not play out the way you had hoped.

Forming and maintaining that internship program was a labor of love and it came with its own forms of ups and downs, but more often than not, the program allowed us to have first pick of the most promising people that we already knew we wanted to hire into their first job out of college.

If this makes any sense for your organization, I can't recommend enough the value you might find through establishing a relationship with the schools in your area. The benefits are both in the access to the pool of fresh talent you'll find, as well as the energy you'll *get back* as you *give back* with your knowledge and experience to those who will be the future of our industry. For us, we started with the professors and career counselors by just asking what the students needed and they did a lot of the heavy lifting to shape our initial program. Start with the people closest to the students and be prepared to listen to what they tell you!

The second benefit from our relationship with the universities was the flow of new business referrals they came with! Many small businesses reach out to the programs and professors at their local schools for fresh, affordable marketing help. Because of our internship as well as a healthy communication channel, often that meant the schools were sending the requests our way.

Similarly, many of our employees brought with them a network of people they knew who needed marketing services. We filled our early client list with many of the family, neighbors, friends, and favorite businesses of our employees. And you know that at that early stage, we were grateful for every piece of business that came our way! Especially clients that seemingly fell into our laps through our interns sharing what they were doing with their network of contacts.

Past Performance is No Guarantee of Future Success

This was a great starting point, working with so many new and different clients from a broad range of industries. And it was invaluable in helping us learn about the business we were in and the type of work we were great at. We also learned the work we did not do well and the types of clients that we did not enjoy working with.

Looking back it's obvious, but I've seen it now many times in my consulting that companies in the early stages of business say "yes" to just about everything that comes along. This leads to doing lots of different things for lots of different clients—usually in a very one-off and inefficient way—as the company strives to satisfy any (or all!) needs expressed by the client. Afterall, it's a paying client, right? They don't just grow on trees! So we over-delivered, over-served, under-charged, and typically, found our efforts under-appreciated.

I've observed that it takes about three years on average for a company to figure out who they are. This includes deciding what they do and who they can best serve. More on this in Part 2, but at some point, typically around year three, almost all business owners are forced to take a look at what they've done, how they've done it, and who they've done it for, then begin to make more deliberate decisions about who they serve and how they want to serve them.

But this decision should not be forced and cannot be made final without reaching several significant milestones of success and failure, elation, disillusionment, and gaining a bit of perspective.

Schröder's Staircase at Work

There is an optical illusion called the "Schröder Stairs Ambiguous Figure" made famous by M.C. Escher, that shows many staircases linking together in beautifully rendered repeating patterns, but if your eye tries to follow any of the stairs, you are brain-wrenchingly drawn to a point where you can no longer tell if you're climbing up or going down.

I've found Schröder's Staircase to be a great analogy for where we were during year three of our business, and for most of the client agencies I've worked with at some point in their history.

For us, things were fine. The work was good, problems came and went, and we learned and improved, but it was unexciting. The four partners had settled into a groove where we each had small, easily managed, but disparate teams totaling a couple dozen employees.

We were on track to bill about $2 million that year and sales were pretty much flat.

We bounced between 60 to 80 clients most of that year, and we would add one or two most months, but we would also lose one or two most months, typically through no fault of our own. You know, clients just come and go.

We weren't climbing up, but we weren't going down.

We didn't really stress client retention as we were well above the "industry norm" – an abysmal 30% and an average of 4-6 months for digital marketers at the time – and we told ourselves their departure was not our fault; clients can be fickle.

So, that's where we'd gotten to when we were suddenly faced by the problem that woke us up to one of life's painful, inevitable facts—*nothing lasts forever!*

We had been running a profitable business, but we were not pursuing growth and we were not planning ahead for when things would change. Though we knew they inevitably would.

Why weren't we prepared for this?

The Enemy of Great is "Good Enough"

Business owners seem to believe the ideal for their business is to have everything running smoothly. Unfortunately, we often learn the hard way that the times when things are "going along just fine" are always temporary and may even be disguising areas of the business that need to be reviewed, improved, or completely removed.

Management guru Peter Drucker is famously quoted as saying, "What gets measured, gets managed." Essentially, you get what you're looking for and you focus on what you have the data and ability to affect.

I recently learned there was more to this quote. Drucker originally followed the oft-quoted opener by adding, "Even when it's pointless to measure and manage it, and even if it harms the organization to do so."

We were managing by what we could measure and all the indicators at hand were telling us things were fine. But business is like a tree that is strengthened by hard weather to thicken its branches and deepen its roots.

It is during these times when things are going well that I've found business owners tend to relax, schedule their vacations, or get caught up in side projects and distractions. Now, I'm all for relaxation, vacations, and side projects, but it's the job of the business owner primarily to protect and plan against dangers to the business. Even if that danger comes in the form of complacency with everything running smoothly and the business being "good enough".

World-renowned business analyst Jay Abraham says, "You are surrounded by simple, obvious solutions that can dramatically increase your income, power, influence and success. The problem is you just don't see them."

Fortunately, he also says, "As soon as you open your mind to doing things differently, the doors of opportunity practically fly off their hinges."

So, what is stopping your company from being a great company? It's probably being a "pretty good" company. For our company, we had simply not made the decision to become anything more than what we'd become.

Decide to Re-Decide

In retrospect, it's easy to see—and embarrassing to admit. We were not running a great business. *We weren't even trying to run a great business!* We had grown complacent, apathetic even, and were content to run the business the way it had been going, with no real thought of the future beyond the next quarter's goals for revenue and retention.

We weren't thinking long-term.

Your business may be stuck thinking short-term like we were, or you may be running a long-term venture with a multi-generational business plan. While studying in Asia, I learned that many Japanese companies, called *Shinise*, are built on one-thousand-year business plans. This still amazes me. Contrast that with the American company's average "lifespan" of less than 20 years! And the startling Bureau of Labor statistic that one in five U.S. businesses fail within the first year and five out of ten will fail within 5 years. With a 50% failure rate in the first five years, it's no wonder so many business owners aren't making one-thousand-year business plans!

Your business may only be looking at that twenty-year timeline for its definition of success. In fact, many owners I speak with are glad to have had a two-decade run! Or you may be looking for a cash-out or quick flip that is built and sold within 3-5 years. There's no right or wrong answer—except to have no plan at all!

With our client list of "business sellers," I've learned it's absolutely critical that you operate from a minimum of a 3-year business plan. But you can look forward to more on this in Part 2!

For my company, the imminent departure of one of our principals was the wakeup call we needed to re-evaluate where we were, what we had become, and where we wanted our business to go. We had a decision to make; actually, we found we had many decisions we needed to *re-make* and three very important questions we needed to answer in order to get a plan in place and regenerate our lost momentum.

3½ Questions to answer when planning the sale of your business:

1. What is our business worth today?
2. What do we need it to be worth for us to exit?
3. How long would it take to get there?

And once we knew the answer to these three questions, we found ourselves asking another, final question:

    3½. What did we need to do to get there the fastest way possible?

For us, the clock was already ticking.

Chapter 3 – Why You Should Sell Your Business

All things are born to die.

Yes, I'm starting this chapter out by confronting you with the very real, very morbid contemplation of death.

And if that wasn't enough, I'm gonna go one further by pulling out a quote from the Dalai Lama—

> "If from the beginning your attitude is 'Yes, death is part of our lives,' then it may be easier to face."
> –From *The Dalai Lama's Book of Wisdom*
> by Dalai Lama XIV

I'm not being morose to point out that in the context of your business, it will eventually come to an end. Paraphrasing the Roman emperor and Stoic philosopher Marcus Aurelius, "Consider how impermanent all mortal things are. Remember death. Remember that you [and your business, eventually] will die."

So, if we know an ending is inevitable, why not plan now for how you'd like that ending to happen? Just plan on the death of your business and work out the details in advance.

I've talked to too many business owners who look at the business they own as an extension of themselves. It's back to focusing too much on the "own" in business ownership.

By remembering that all things have both beginnings and endings, we can separate ourselves and our individual future from the business and its future.

As I've said before, the first and most critical step of selling a business is to leave behind the mindset of owning that business and the identity that comes with being the "business owner" to instead become the seller of a business that you own.

In this way, we don't attach so much importance to the thing itself, but rather have the distance and perspective to see our role simply as having ownership of something that someone else wants to buy.

The Metaphor of the Family Car

In other areas of our lives, we all recognize that the moment you buy something, you're also taking on the end-result of that purchase.

When you buy a house, you buy the need to insure, furnish, and maintain it.

When you buy takeout food, you also buy the requirement to throw the cups and wrappers in the trash.

To really communicate to my clients this mindset that

being a business owner means you are creating something someone wants to buy, I use the metaphor of the family car.

When you buy a family car, there's really three possible outcomes:

> **Scenario #1** – You sell it and lose money. This is the result we're all most familiar with.
>
> **Scenario #2** – You give it away to someone (and lose all of the money).
>
> **Scenario #3** – You drive that car into the ground and it's not worth anything to anybody.

In our metaphor comparing your business to the family car, scenario #1 would mean you "used up" (see the accounting definition of "utility") the value of the car and sold it for the remainder of the value (the accounting definition of "depreciating an asset") to someone who found it in acceptable condition and was willing to pay for the remaining utility of the car.

In business, this would be selling it in a liquidation sale for the cost of the underlying assets or, in a service business, for the amount of current annual billing, often called "1X" or one-times the book of business.

Scenario #2 – Giving it to someone might be passing the car on to a son or daughter who is going off to school, or to a younger driver who needs transportation and would value the vehicle despite its "used" status.

For your business, this would be a family or employee transition plan, typically involving you and some of the ownership team staying on as mentors or board members to ease the transferal of the leadership role. Rarely is any money made and this most often leads to two people getting paid for doing the same job for a period of time.

Most critically, though, no money is made! It's a net cost to transition the company.

Scenario #3, "driving the car into the ground" is the graphic expression of using up all the value and ending with burying the now "lifeless" vehicle in a plot of ground. This is another common scenario for cars, to just end up as unusable junk at the end of their lifespan, but sadly, it's also a scenario I see playing out with the owners of service businesses.

I've talked to business owners who say, "I've had a good run. I built a great business and it benefitted me when I needed it. The business allowed me to take care of my family and put my kids through school. Now I'll just take down my shingle and quit the business."

This is nothing less than closing-up shop and with nothing to show for it! I hope this horrifies you as much as it does me.

It's a shameful way to just give up and throw it all away, and I weep and tremble when I hear about these scenarios. It pains me to know there are business owners who see such little value in the work of their hands—the value, brand, relationships, and impact they've made with their business, no matter how big, profitable, long-lived, or geographically spread, are too great to be so simply dismissed and devalued.

I present to you a different outcome from those above. Scenario #4: Selling it for more than you believed it was worth.

But is that possible? Is that more than just wishful thinking?

In our car metaphor, this would be the equivalent of taking great care of a classic vehicle. A vintage or rare model that has been well-maintained or restored actually goes up in value rather than being a depreciating asset in the portfolio of the vehicle owner.

For example, a Ford GT40 MK II, the model of car that famously beat Ferrari in the 1966 Le Mans race featured in the film *Ford v Ferrari* went for $9.8 million at auction in 2018. That's a lot more than the few thousand dollars one of the original cars cost to build!

In the business world, this means creating a company that has exactly the right "parts and upgrades" so that it will have more value to the buyer than the original owner. The term for this is a "strategic acquisition."

That is what you should be creating with your business—a vehicle that not only took you where you wanted to go, but took you there in style, and, ultimately, when sold to the right buyer, took care of you even afterward by selling for much more than you believed it was worth.

Wanting to Sell Your Business

I said before that creating a business you can sell is actually the act of creating a business someone else wants to buy. Taking this further, this is also an act of making your business *worth enough* that you'd want to sell it.

The business owners I talk to that don't want to sell are simply saying, "It's worth more to me than to someone else, so I might as well keep it."

This thinking is exactly right!

I do not believe selling a business should be a losing scenario or even a situation of the owner saying, "I'll take what I can get."

You already know how strongly I feel about the role of a "business owner." Because you own the business, you're the one fully responsible to make the business worth enough that you WANT to sell it.

Remember my three and a half questions from when we needed to decide to rebuild, exit, or abandon my company? Let's revisit them.

3½ Questions to answer when planning the sale of your business:

1. What is our business worth today?
2. What do we need it to be worth?
3. How long will it take to get there?
3½. What do we need to do to get there as fast as possible?

You need the answers to those questions now, starting with knowing the current valuation of your business. Then you need to know "your number" – what is the amount of money that you need to see, both at the deal level and the personal level, to make this worth your time. (Because selling the business is work, you'd better make sure you like what you're getting paid for doing that work!)

Then, you need to identify the delta between what it's worth now and what it needs to be worth for you to want to sell it. At this point, it's simply a matter of determining what steps you need to take in the business to cross that

delta and make the business worth the amount you want to sell for to the right buyer.

This step in Exit Planning is called Value Creation.

Value Creation and Exit Planning

I don't believe you can sell a business for more than it's worth. That would be dishonest and misrepresentative. But I do believe that value is relative. So, the goal of selling a business is to find a buyer who values it as much or more than you value it.

Through the act of creating a company that someone wants to buy, you are, by the inverse definition, creating a company that someone wants to own.

So, you'd never sell the business to someone who values

it less than you, and in the act of working to sell it, it may just turn out that the person who wants to own the business is you!

I've seen this play out more than a few times with clients who originally gave us their exit number, but it was not their real number, it was too low. Or it was their real number at the time, but then their situation changed.

The owner of a California agency that specialized in web design had gone from doing all of the coding and design himself as a glorified freelancer to finally having a team in place doing the work and decided that he was happier staying on as the CEO, stating, "I finally have my dream job. Why would I want to sell it to someone else?"

Why, indeed. The by-product of creating a business that others want to own is that you've created a great business for anyone to own. As an aside, I was obligated to tell him that he's just delaying the inevitable...

Queue Marcus Aurelius and the Dalai Lama.

Chapter 4 – The Role of Value Creation

If through value creation, your best-case scenario is to sell the company for your goal price (or better), the worst-case scenario is that when you finally have the company in a place where you could sell it, you may end up as the owner of a company you no longer want to sell!

Okay, true worst worst-case is you cannot sell the business, but in that scenario, I have to ask, are you any worse off than you found yourself at the beginning? If today you own an unsellable company and you work for a year (or years) to improve it only to end up with a better version of the same unsellable company, doesn't that just mean you haven't completed the steps of value creation for your eventual exit?

SPOILER ALERT: At the end of this book, and at the end of nearly every story of a company exit (successful or even failed), you will find there are just two levers for the owner to pull: timeline and total price.

In order to make a company that *someone else* would want to own, you are first making a company that *you* would want to own.

Before building my own agency, I worked in advertising for over twelve years at four different agencies, so I saw the inner workings and different business models they were using to serve and bill their clients.

What I learned was that most agencies were actually bad at finding the right clients to work with and knowing who they should be working with and what they should be doing.

Start with Who

In my dozen years of work with agencies, and the initial three years of my own agency, I found that agency owners were usually chasing after clients they couldn't handle, didn't know how to manage, or really shouldn't have been working with in the first place.

I also saw that each agency thought they were unique and special, but they were offering services that were largely commoditized and mostly undifferentiated in the minds of their clients. That's hard news to hear.

Worst of all, I saw that too many agency people undervalued what they did, charged too little, over-delivered for the clients, did too much work for the price, and generally bent themselves out of shape to try to serve or meet all of the dramatic and fast-changing needs of the client.

These are all exactly the *worst* parts of running a service business and the reason most people assume you can't *sell* a business for more than the value of the client list—

or the almost standard "3x EBITDA"—because it's just a *"job"* or a list of services that someone has to go and fulfill.

That all changes when you go through the self-discovery and decision-making process I have come to call the Automatic Exit Framework.

The Automatic Exit Framework

We'll go through it in depth in Part 2 of this book, but it begins when you come to the realization that you can't be everything to everybody and you figure out who you are (and aren't) supposed to be working with.

With this knowledge, you drill down on what the customer actually needs and how you can become the best in the world at delivering that specific result—while stopping all other services!

Then, you get the processes and people right inside of the business so that you're ready to grow and scale the business.

At that point, you turn on the best marketing machine in the world (that's coming up in Part 2) to line up your exact ideal prospects and have them raise their hands to work with you.

Finally, if you haven't already, it's time to fire the clients that no longer fit the business you're in, as well as any people who are not onboard or required for the future of the business. And, by the way, as one of those people, you'll be firing yourself! (Also coming up in Part 2.) Among the people no longer needed to deliver the service to your clients, that *must* include you! Don't worry, you'll have other responsibilities, just not client deliverables.

When properly situated, there's no room in the organization's operations for a person called a "business owner."

Remember, we talked about this? The only job of a business owner is to be outside of the business, improving it from the strategic level, and this is the only allowable role if you hope to transition into becoming that rare and magical creature called a "business seller."

Becoming a Business Seller

You must stop being a "business owner" and become a "business seller."

How does that sound?

Is that what you want for yourself?

Do you see how having a path like the Automatic Exit Framework could help you know both where to take your business and the fastest way to get there?

It will. It's what I wish I'd known when I'd been challenged to sell our agency with only a nine-month countdown, and what I've taught to hundreds of agency owners since then.

Are you ready to see how the Automatic Exit Framework can be implemented for your business? Let's dive in!

PART 2 – The Automatic Exit Framework

In Part 1, I compared building your business to going on a journey. We talked about departing the well-traveled road to follow the less-traveled path of your unique business, including identifying the Trail Markers that got you to the place you ended up. Now, let's look forward at the place where you want to go in this journey and the people who are going to help you get there.

The Automatic Exit Framework will walk you through the adjustments in your thinking and the decisions in your business that you'll need to make to fully complete the process of going from a "business owner" to being a "business seller" and ultimately reaching your goal of being a person who has (past tense) *sold* the business successfully with the least pain and for the most money.

This is the simplest way to walk you through the ten steps to achieve your own Automatic Exit for your business.

The Automatic Exit Framework – Step 1: Decide Who You Serve

In mapping the course you want to follow, it's as

important to decide where you *don't* want to go as it is to decide where you want to arrive. I tell clients that it's as essential going forward to know which doors to close as which ones they want to keep open. Sometimes in life and for your business, there's nothing more distracting than an open door.

An important decision on this journey, then, is deciding the types of clients you will focus on and those you will no longer work with. And I *mean* you'll no longer be working with them!

I mentioned before that it's typically a gradual process over a period of time, usually about year three, for a business to develop their own identity of who they are, what they do, and who they best serve.

When I first get involved, most businesses are still taking clients from wherever they can get them, especially if they're coming in by referrals or word-of-mouth.

And I'll tell you what you already know, that there's nothing better than having new clients come to you through these channels. Getting clients by referral and word-of-mouth means that you're doing great work for your clients. It's a huge compliment and mark of approval for your business. And don't get me wrong, these types of new clients are typically the easiest to close, they come in at your best prices, and they often don't even shop you around or look at competitors. But, on the downside, getting clients through this channel is your least reliable, least controllable, least scalable, and least long-term method of new client acquisition.

We'll cover in Step 6 how to establish the best method in the world for your business development, but at this stage we want to start by simply asking some questions and making decisions:

1. Who have been your best customers in the past?
2. What industries or niches have you had the most success in?
3. What specific case studies do you have that convey the type of work you're best at doing?

Then, after asking and answering these three questions, I get a little bit dangerous—*maybe even a little crazy!*—by introducing the "L" word into a business conversation... but I would ask you with genuine interest in your answer:

3½. What customers do you *love* working with?

What's Love Got to Do with It?

Can you really work with customers you love?

Yes! You really can. And why shouldn't you?

It's your business and you will eventually be spending hours and hours of your own time, thought, and energy on these customers. So, if you can choose to work with anybody on the planet, why not choose to work with people you would love to deal with every day?

Won't that almost guarantee that you'll be bringing great energy and doing your best work?

Now, some people love working with real estate agents

or mortgage lenders. Some really love the professional services industry or health and med spa owners. I had a client that loved working with the marketing teams at credit unions to rebuild their brands!

I say bless his heart.

If you're like I was, you may hear these examples and be thinking, "there's no amount of money you could pay me to work with that audience," but that's actually the great news! That's why we all have different businesses and can focus on serving different people.

So, if you're honest with yourself and your team and you answer those three (and a half!) questions, you should identify one group that fits the criteria of a great audience for your business.

Pick One Audience

Chances are you may have several groups, but it is critical to pick just one and narrow your marketing efforts to just that group for the exercises that are to follow. If you need help deciding on that audience, additional questions that may help you narrow your choice are:

1. Can they afford your services?
2. Are there enough of them to keep growing your business?
3. Is there growth in that industry for the future of their businesses?
4. Do I know this industry well enough to confidently step in and solve their biggest problem?

The Automatic Exit Framework – Step 2: Solve the Biggest Problem

Now you have picked the audience you want to serve. Congratulations! That is a huge first step. Next, you're going to solve the biggest problem that audience faces.

Simple, right?

I've found that there are 4 types of service businesses:

1. Unfocused – The first type is unfocused, doing whatever for whoever. This is what I went through with my agency in the beginning, and I commonly see this during the startup phase of most businesses.
2. Client-focused – Busy, busy, busy doing whatever the clients require. This is a natural evolution for most businesses, but it is *still* unfocused and has always proven to be unsustainable.
3. Skills-focused – Busy, busy, busy doing the things *the business* is good at. This is typically based on the skills of one person (usually the founder) or one or more members of the team.
4. Result-focused – Developing a service (or set of services) that deliver a desired result. This is a business that is consistently, predictably providing one specific result for *only* the clients that need it.

Automatic Exit: Turn Your Service Business into a Sellable Asset

You'll notice in the 4th type, they are not doing type 2 & 3 activities, chasing neither the clients' needs or the abilities of the current team. This is the most cost-efficient, intrinsically motivated, and, you guessed it, the most *sellable* type of service business.

Think about it in your own experience. When your car won't start, that becomes your biggest problem. It doesn't matter that the front tire is low on air, or the gas tank is half full. You need a new car battery! Well, you really need a jump start—but then you're probably going to need a new car battery.

When you need a car battery, you're going to go to an auto parts store because they specialize in batteries. Do they sell batteries at other stores? Yes. I happen to know they sell them at Costco (of course they do, they sell everything at Costco), but when you think of where to *buy* a car battery, you think first of an auto parts store. And maybe even a specific auto parts store near you, a NAPA or an O'Reilly's. That's the place you go because it's what you think of first when you're suddenly forced into a "car battery shopping" situation.

What about an oil change? Any mechanic can change your oil, but Jiffy Lube has built a $500 million business by being the top-of-mind place for so many people to get a fast oil change.

Now think pizza. Most any chef can cook up a pizza and there are millions of restaurants that serve it, but there's one chain that's focused on having a low-cost pizza that's "hot and ready." And Little Caesar's has grown to be a $4.25 billion franchise because of its highly specific offer.

You want your business to be the place your ideal customers think of first when they're suddenly in a situation where they need your service. You need to specialize in providing one specific solution to your target audience's biggest problem.

One Specific Result

A new car battery. A fast oil change. A "hot and ready" pizza. Do you offer one specific solution for your clients?

Not yet? Start by thinking about your target audience and ask yourself what their biggest problem is. Ask the members of your team. If you're close to the audience, this is easier to do. If you don't know what the biggest problem is, start listing all their problems, then rank them from biggest to smallest. Pick the biggest one you can solve.

If you're still looking for this problem, invite feedback from the audience itself. Email out the list you created of all their problems and ask them which is their biggest. You could also run an ad asking for this feedback. If you already have customers in this target audience, have a conversation to survey them on their biggest problem.

For Jiffy Lube, the biggest problem is that their customers want a fast, low-cost oil change. In the strangest sentence I may ever write, I'll state that:

Little Caesar's is not much different from Jiffy Lube.

Am I right? Their customers want a fast, low-cost solution to their biggest problem. For them, it's not an oil change, it's a "hot and ready" pizza.

Determine what your customers want the most and then provide one specific solution to their biggest problem. And the solution has to be so specific that when they run into that problem, they think of you. Plus, this level of specificity will allow you to focus all of your marketing on the problem that they have and the solution you provide.

Sell Them What They Want, Deliver What They Need

Often, your prospect does not know what they need. They may know what they *want*, but that may not be the actual result or service that they need.

For example, my company Relevant Business Development sells a business development system—an entire process that you can put in place in your own business that "flips the script" so you automatically get the clients that you want to work with reaching out to you.

The prospect says they want us to get them new customers.

Here's what we actually give them: a biz dev system set up inside their *own* business to make them get their *own* leads and *own* their own new business pipeline. I know, that's a lot of "owning!"

But as the Rolling Stones taught us, you can't always get what you want, but you *can* get what you need.

We give clients ownership of their own lead pipeline because it is what we've learned the prospect *needs*.

But I don't sell it that way. We sell them what they *want*.

The prospects we talk to for that business say that they *want* new customers. They've seen myriad offers in the marketplace saying "I guarantee 50, 100, or 1,000 leads per month, day, or minute" and they think that's what they must want.

But nobody wants hundreds or thousands of leads, or worse, someone else's definition of what a "good lead" looks like. What they want is new customers every month coming into the business and paying full price for their product or service. So, we sell them what they want, and then actually deliver what they need. Again, hat tip to Mick and Keith for their sound advice.

So, what does your audience want? And what do they actually need?

What is their biggest problem?

I've seen businesses that say they provide "advertising services." Or "promotional strategies." Or even "marketing solutions."

I really hate the term "solutions." What does that even mean?

Could they be more vague?

If you hadn't already noticed it, now that I point it out, you'll start seeing it everywhere. Is it on your own website? What do they mean by "solutions"? "You've got problems, we sell solutions!" Just tell them what the solution is, don't make people guess.

Instead of "services," "strategies," and "solutions," tell them the result you sell that they're looking for. And again, be very specific.

I mentioned Relevant Business Development sells a system that generates new, qualified customers that are the client's ideal prospects. That "system" provides the result the customer is buying.

Separately, with my consulting I deliver the framework and exact process to sell a service business for the most money. (Yes, that's the book you're reading right now.) That is the biggest problem that my target audience wants to solve. That "process" provides the result the customer is buying: selling their business.

For another example, what ultimately led to the multi-million-dollar valuation of my previous agency is that we targeted our service at a new audience—ad agencies—where we understood their biggest problem was to deliver digital marketing at a high quality for the lowest cost. We didn't say, "We can do SEO, PPC, social media content, and digital ads better than anyone else in the world."

Our pitch was much more simple. Pay attention to this part! This was our pitch:

1. We asked them what they charged for the digital marketing services they currently offered.
2. We quoted the price that we could provide those services to them for and explained that our low cost was because of our much lower billable rate.
3. We told them they should start charging their clients more, then pay us our price to do the work, and keep the difference.
4. If our pricing was lower (and it always was) and they could be charging more (and they always could), it made sense to switch over to using our service for their clients.

We solved the biggest problem we could for them with our one specific result. They weren't confident in their ability to charge more and make money with the digital marketing services they currently offered, so we took all the risk off of them and gave them our guaranteed lower rates with a white-labeled service.

And because we niched down and specialized in working with just ad agencies, we were able to become the best in the world at what we did for our customers.

The Automatic Exit Framework – Step 3: Be the Best in the World

If you want to become the best in the world at what you do, there are two ways to do it. First, I'll share the hard way.

The hard way to be the best in the world at something is to be born with all of the innate talent you need to be better and outpace everyone else—*every other person currently living on the planet!*

Or outwork them. Or know something they don't and put in years to develop the expertise required to be the very best at it. Or all of the above.

I'll use the example of Michael Phelps, the 28-time Olympic medalist in swimming. He is undeniably the best in the world at what he does, but on top of the genetic physical traits he was born with, he put in countless hours of training and preparation with the best coaches and tools in the world to achieve his status. Does that sound hard? It is!

Now, I'll share the easy way.

Niche down. Become so specific and specialized in what you do that there is no one else doing it.

I helped an ad agency become the best in the world at doing full rebranding for national and large regional credit unions that needed a brand refresh.

Were there other people doing that work? Certainly. But were any of them so narrowly focused on it that they became the best in the world? Not that I know of. So, it was easy to advertise that promise and deliver on that service. And that's all you need to be able to do to be the best in the world for your client.

Do Your One Thing

Little Caesar's became the best in the world at what they do because they're focused on the one thing they do—provide a "hot and ready" pizza. Now you might point out that they sell other things. You're right, they have crazy bread and sauces, sodas, and some locations sell chicken wings, but I would emphasize that they're not advertising themselves as the provider of all those other things. They're marketing is all focused on the cheap and fast "hot and ready" pizza that sticks in the mind of the customer. Pun intended.

Jiffy Lube became number one best in the world at what they do because it's the one thing they choose to focus on. They are world famous for a 10-minute oil change. Did you even know they do other things? I went to their website and found out they also offer battery, brakes, engine, and tire services along with 23 other things that *aren't* a fast oil change.

That tells you they picked one thing to focus on and became the best in the world at doing that one thing. Or at least, they became *best known* in the world for doing that thing. As long as we're learning lessons from some of the best-known companies in the world, why don't we take a look at the playbook for another number one company, McDonald's.

The Automatic Exit Framework – Step 4: Make it McDonald's

When examining the world's most successful fast-food chain, let's first acknowledge that we've bitten off a lot with these ten steps that will help you implement the Automatic Exit Framework into your business.

Now, before we sink our teeth into this next bite, let's take a look at what we've covered in steps 1 through 3 that led us up to this significant fourth step.

So far, you've decided who you want to serve. You've determined what their biggest problem is and how exactly you can solve it for them. And you've made the decision to do the exact, specific thing you do for your ideal client better than anyone else in the world.

That's a great start! Now we're ready for the next step.

To make your agency business into a sellable asset, you have to "make it McDonald's." This is my punchy and more memorable way of saying "turn every aspect of your business into a replicable process that is so simple you could basically hire teenagers to do it."

See how that just doesn't make a great chapter heading?

The business professor in me loves this story from *Rich Dad, Poor Dad* where the author, Robert Kiyosaki, tells of a teacher that asked the class to raise their hand if they could make a better hamburger than McDonald's. Just about every hand in the class went up ... Right? Most have us can make a much better tasting hamburger on our grill at home. So how is McDonald's the most successful food chain in the world? Because McDonald's isn't actually successful at making the best tasting hamburger. So, what does McDonald's do that they're the best in the world at doing?

The process.

McDonald's is the best in the world at effectively reproducing the process of making their unique hamburger. In business, we call these "standard operating procedures" or SOPs and McDonald's is so good at creating a standardized process for each aspect of their franchise that you can go to Paris, Rio, or Beijing and get a Big Mac (or a Jù wú bà in Mandarin), and it will be a similar experience. I know, I've done it! In the name of research, of course.

And, what's even more impressive is that your experience will be delivered by a low-cost employee, typically a teenager being paid minimum wage, and yet it will be virtually identical. This further speaks to the power of having a system and replicable processes in place that make it easy to deliver the same promised level of quality over and over and over.

So, how do we take an agency business and "make it McDonald's"? We help our clients create SOPs for each area and deliverable of their business.

Create Your Business SOPs

You start by making these as specific as possible. Read through the Example SOP, then go and do this for one of your own business processes.

First, name the process by the result you are about to standardize. Then, follow the template to explain each step of the process in terms even a teenage hourly worker could follow.

EXAMPLE SOP: Client Project Review Script

>**PROCESS: Client Project Review Script**
>**RESULT: The business will have a general script for client conversations regarding project reviews.**
>
>**OVERVIEW: First and throughout, remember the purpose of the conversation is to connect with the client, to follow up or get feedback on previous work, to capture information about current or future work, and to convey that our agency listens, understands and is capable of helping the client to achieve their goals.**
>- The length of the conversation should be flexible to the client's expectations, but the recommended total conversation should be 15 to 20 minutes.
>- Please capture all of your notes for this conversation on the Client Project Review form and submit it to the Account Manager and the team.
>
>**Client Conversation Script**
>*To serve as a guideline for client conversations and to facilitate information pass-along to internal teams.*

- Opening
    - Use pleasantries and small talk to open all conversations. Be calm and relaxed and remember that our business is about relationships. Our clients do business with us because we are their partner and friend.
        - Ask about common interests, co-workers, upcoming personal plans.
        - Record important notes about client and contacts for future conversations.
- Past Project Review
    - Briefly (2-5 minutes) ask client how recent projects went or are performing.
        - Example: "Is everything going great with (specific project)?"
        - Record positive or negative feedback and report it to your team.
- Current Project Review
    - Introduce or review current project with the client. Use project development materials from team.
    - Recap where the project stands and review the timeline with specific dates for deliverables by both the agency and the client.
        - Ask about changes in expectations, deadlines, or scope of the project.
        - Record any action steps mentioned by the client.
- Conversation Summary
    - Summarize the feedback the client gave on previous projects.
        - Example "I'm glad to hear that (last project) is going/went well.
    - Review Action Steps discussed.
        - Example "So, I have down that we're going to get new artwork to you by Thursday."

- ▪ Ask client: "Does this match what you want us to work on?"
- <u>Closing</u>
  - ○ Say "thank you" and review any personal information discussed, especially up-coming plans or out-of-office events.
    - ▪ Example: "And have a nice vacation next week. We'll take care of things so that you can enjoy some time away."
    - ▪ If applicable, set up appointment for next phone conversation.

Afterward: Immediately following the conversation, complete the form and email it out to the internal team. Send a recap summary to the client if any changes were introduced.

Done correctly, you have a process and even a script that can be handed to anyone with little or no training and it can be replicated. With each SOP, you're codifying and documenting "the right way" that your business does business.

The example above became the way our agency handled client conversations, which for us was a monthly activity that happened the same with each client no matter which employee was running that call. And, because it was systematized, we got better at doing it and could have meaningful trainings and improve these conversations inside of the organization.

Compare that to just letting our people get on phone calls and try to help the clients. That lack of a system leads to too great of a reliance on individual performers being exceptional at what they do, or of having "good days" on the job, or a good rapport with a specific client.

Too many variables leads to a high risk of not delivering a consistent and replicable process that produces the same quality of result on a consistent and reliable basis.

Imagine ordering a Big Mac in China and finding that the person behind the counter just makes it the way she likes it and doesn't follow the SOP defined by the company? She might be a trained chef that delivers a better-than-expected hamburger, and it would still be "wrong" because it's not a McDonald's hamburger, and that is what the customer at the restaurant has paid to receive.

Automatic Exercise

Go through the processes and deliverables that make up your company's "Best in the World" service offer and create an SOP for each one.

Again, the goal here is to make it so simple that the least training possible could allow any employee with the right tools to be able to deliver a consistent experience.

Like in our example, start by defining the task, deliverable, or outcome that you're about to standardize. We recommend including screenshots, video, charts, and references along with each SOP so that the finished resource has all of the information necessary to complete that individual process.

Good and Bad SOPs

An SOP can be completely spelled out and still be bad for your business. In *The Checklist Manifesto*, Atul Gawande teaches that there are good checklists and bad.

> "Bad checklists are vague and imprecise. They are too long; they are hard to use; they are impractical. They are made by desk jockeys with no awareness of the situations in which they are to be deployed. They treat the people using the tools as dumb and try to spell out every single step. They turn people's brains off rather than turn them on.
>
> "Good checklists, on the other hand, are precise. They are efficient, to the point, and easy to use even in the most difficult situations. They do not try to spell out everything—a checklist cannot fly a plane. Instead, they provide reminders of only the most critical and important steps—the ones that even the highly skilled professionals using them could miss. Good checklists are, above all, practical."
>
> — Atul Gawande, *The Checklist Manifesto: How to Get Things Right*

After you've written the SOP, ensure that it is not Gawande's definition of a bad checklist by having someone actually go through the process following the list. Best of all, hand it to someone not familiar with your process and see how they do. The best SOPs are those that guide the process to keep it specific and efficient without spelling out every step to the exclusion of making it effective.

When you've created SOPs that make your business processes so replicable that you've made it McDonald's, you'll need to have the right people doing the right jobs for your company and customers. This is where we get into having the right people doing their best work and a little extended metaphor about a bus.

The Automatic Exit Framework – Step 5: Assign Seats

In *Good to Great*, Jim Collins introduced us all to the concept of "getting the right people on the bus." He helps clarify business priorities in his highly influential study of top performing companies by explaining business building with a metaphor of a bus trip.

> "The executives who ignited the transformations from good to great did not first figure out where to drive the bus and then get people to take it there. No, they FIRST got the right people on the bus (and the wrong people off the bus) and THEN figured out where to drive it.
>
> They said, in essence, 'Look, I don't really know where we should take this bus. But I know this much: If we get the right people on the bus, the right people in the right seats, and the wrong people off the bus, then we'll figure out how to take it someplace great.'"
>
> — Jim Collins, *Good to Great*

If you're seeing this again after a while, or you're somehow reading about this for the first time, let's just pause for a moment and take in the brilliance of it.

You don't have to know where you're going when you start the trip. Find the right people that work together and provide a beneficial result for the client, and you'll figure out where the bus needs to go.

So, let's see who's on the bus. I want us to look at your org chart.

Go ahead and grab yours.

I'll wait.

I hope we're both laughing and you're pausing here to go and actually pull out your diagram of organizational hierarchy, titles, and responsibilities.

What I hope you're not doing is cringing with the guilt of having run this long in your business without an org chart!

Even if it's not current or "comprehensive," you need to be operating with an org chart. Next to your financial statements and 3-year plan, this is the most critical document we use in the creation of growth, scale, and exit plans for our client list of successful business sellers.

Now here's what I know: your org chart is wrong. Not that it isn't current or accurate, hopefully it is, but that you have altogether the wrong titles for an organization your size.

Automatic Quiz

Do you have a COO? Are they actually doing the job of a COO? This is the classic title creep. I'm happy to help you answer this for yourself. Here is a generally accepted job description for a COO:

> A Chief Operating Officer is typically employed at large or mid-size corporations as the second-in-command on their company's executive team who oversees all of an organization's activities and ensures that the existing business infrastructure has the capacity to achieve the company's strategic goals.
>
> COOs hire and train business administrators who create organized systems for completing their department's key functions. Their role is to identify the essential structure of the

business and assess its efficiency as the company grows and are the main point of contact for their company's key suppliers.

From: https://www.indeed.com/hire/job-description/coo-chief-operating-officer

Here is a generally accepted job description for a Director of Operations:

Directors of Operations typically work for corporations across industries to monitor how their organization carries out daily operations. They work closely with department heads and upper management personnel to identify ways to increase sales, employee retention or customer satisfaction.

Their job is to help upper management promote business growth by maximizing company procedures and its relationship with their customers. They may also be responsible for setting budgets or financial goals for individual departments.

Here is a generally accepted job description for an Operations Manager:

Operations Managers serve on a company's leadership team to oversee the performance, efficiencies, and satisfaction of employees. They analyze the company's organizational process and find ways to enhance employees' work quality and productivity.

Operations Managers build operational policies and strategies that keep the organization functioning smoothly. They often collaborate with Human Resources Managers to establish recruiting, training and hiring strategies. They also oversee financial processes, like auditing, reporting and budgeting, to ensure the company stays in great financial standing.

Are some of you having an epiphany?

Is your "COO" actually a glorified Director or Ops Manager? You might have the other problem, that you've got an over-qualified person sitting in too junior a title, but typically we find the opposite to be the case. Like 80% of the time.

The solution is not to fire, demote, or even address this with your COO.

The solution we can wholeheartedly recommend for most situations is to mentally (read as "inside your own mind") make the adjustment to this person being a COO-in-training. Hopefully they are exactly who you need for where the organization is today. And if they're meeting any of the job requirements listed above, it sounds like they're getting the work done.

Find the Six Seats

Now, let's perform this same exercise for each of the positions that you need to run your business. The seats you need in any business are the following, which many of you will recognize from your first semester in business school:

1. **Operations** – This is what the business does. How it "operates," right? This is the most crucial job you want to hand off, preferably to your COO, but as we just covered, the initial responsibilities could be handled at lower levels by other "operations" titles.

2. **Finance** – This is tracking where the money comes from and where the money goes. Ultimately this role is given to a CFO, if not a CPA, Director

of Finance, AP/AR Manager, or a Controller. I personally have had success with outsourcing this to a Fractional CFO when my company was small enough (say, less than 5-10 people).

3. **Sales & Marketing** – This is how you get customers. This could be a CMO or a VP or Director of Sales or Marketing. Along with Operations and Finance, these are the life and blood of your business. With the right skillset, this or Finance responsibilities could remain longest with the CEO. In other words, bring in an Ops Professional ASAP!

4. **Human Resources or "Management"** – This is the people in your business. The management team (C-suite) and the employees at all levels make up the core and culture of the company. A CHRO or VP of People (there are countless similar titles being used for this) comprises a position whose importance depends on the size of your company. To be clear, people are important, it's just not critical to have a "Person of People" as a full-time role in most smaller organizations.

5. **Technology** – This is the tools, hardware, software, and data systems that fuel and support a service business. Depending on the industry you're in or serve, this position, too, is of varying importance. Ultimately, this would be a CTO, but for most companies, a VP of Tech or even a Technology Director will suffice. Especially in the early stages of growth/headcount and, again, with regard to your industry (i.e. – a SaaS company is gonna need a tech guy in the C-suite!).

6. **Strategy** – *The illusive sixth pillar of business!* This is the planning for product, messaging, fulfillment, product development, and all the other aspects that make up the vision and purpose of the company. Though there are companies creating Chief Strategy Officers and other "Think Tank" and planning type roles, this usually began with and ideally should return to and remain with the CEO.

Knowing which seats you have to fill is a crucial first step. But I would push it even further to say you need to know the *type* of person that should fill each seat.

Find the Five Types of People

In my experience, every company needs people who fill these five roles:

1. **Idea Guy**
2. **Legal Guy**
3. **Numbers Guy**
4. **Sales Guy**
5. **Get Stuff Done Guy**

Now, I don't believe these need to be five DIFFERENT guys (or even "guys" at all, so don't get hung up on the gender-specific word choice). What I *do* believe is that these skill sets need to be represented in the company leadership or outsourced to someone that can handle it competently.

Here is what each role should bring to the table:

1. **Idea Guy** needs to have strategic long-term

thinking. This would be a Marketing or Strategic Planning title at a big company. Someone with vision and lots of imagination. He sees opportunities in places that other people haven't even thought to look. When you're like, "What about an online video contest?" he's already saying "And they can call in on their mobile phones and vote for their favorites-- for $.99 per call. Bam! Digital revenue stream."

2. **Legal Guy** needs to love the law. He gets fired up about reading contracts, licensing, intellectual property ins-and-outs and any print smaller than 10 point font. Legal documents, IP/patents, and lawsuits are a common part of business today, so someone at your company needs to love it. I mean LOVE IT!

3. **Numbers Guy** should also be Spreadsheet Guy. He doesn't just like tables, charts and numbers, he has general ledgers printed on his bedsheets. This guy understands that money is making money even when it isn't creating revenue from assets. He does percentages and long-division in his head, can give your company's current cost per sale ratio in his sleep, and feels physical pleasure when the monthly account balances just right.

4. **Sales Guy** is your best friend and your worst enemy. He knows everyone and would rather be on the phone or in a meeting than working alone on his projects. Don't ask him to do paperwork, just let him create relationships and get other people excited about what your company does. The people who are best at this are True

Rainmakers, not salesman-types looking for a quick deal or taking advantage of customers.

5. **Get Stuff Done Guy** is the Executor. It needs done, he finds a way to get it done. He is to a Gantt Chart as a 13-year-old girl is to TikTok. Put him in charge of your projects, your staff or your whole company and he will make sure it all gets done within scope, on time and under budget. Do you need to have a presence at a trade show in Albuquerque in 3 days? Give it to this guy and get out of the way.

Obviously, this was written in an effort to be fun and funny. It's actually from a blogpost I wrote in 2008 while I was in business school (which might still be online somewhere).

But the point I'm making is you want people who are wired to do what they do. That will go above and beyond because they are aligned with their roles and goals, to reference one of Stephen Covey's leadership principles.

I would call these people "PASSIONATE," but that's because I'm a soft/squishy Idea Guy and not a hardline Sales Guy or a straight-shooting Numbers Guy.

Match Personalities to the Seats

I'm a big fan of the personality theories of Myers and Briggs that **group personality types into spectrums across four categories:**

1. **Introversion/Extraversion** – Whether you're inwardly or outwardly focused.
2. **Sensing/Intuition** – How you prefer to take in information.

3. **Thinking/Feeling** – How you prefer to make decisions.
4. **Judging/Perceiving** – How you prefer to live your outer life.

For more on the Myers and Briggs Personality Types, visit 16personalities.com or review the short list in the Appendix.

I hope I'm stating the obvious when I say that certain personality types are better suited for the specific roles of your company. Am I also saying that you should have your people take a personality test and then use that personal information about someone to determine where they might fit into your organization?

Yes. Yes, I am saying that. I've done it and seen many successful organizations do it. And it's similar to the suggestion made by billionaire investor and hedge fund manager Ray Dalio:

> "Imagine if you had baseball cards that showed all the performance stats for your people: batting averages, home runs, errors, ERAs, win/loss records. You could see what they did well and poorly and call on the right people to play the right positions in a very transparent way."
>
> - Ray Dalio, Principles

Dalio created cards for employees that detailed their traits, Meyers-Briggs personality type, as well as their strengths and weaknesses, then used the cards to place his employees in positions to get the most out of them. Famously, Dalio's baseball cards were made available to the executives and department managers at the company, so they were all openly aware of and able to work with the specifics of each person.

Doesn't that strike you as refreshingly different from trying to put any peg into any hole in the org chart? Or worse, situations where everyone seems to know an employee has strengths (and weaknesses), but no one will address it (or fix it)?

Here are my recommendations for the right personality types to hire for each of the Six Seats:

1. **Operations** – Any of the "Analyst" types: Architect (INTJ), Logician (INTP), Commander (ENTJ), or Debater (ENTP)

2. **Finance** – Any of the "Sentinel" types: Logistician (ISTJ), Defender (ISFJ), Executive (ESTJ), or Consul (ESFJ).

3. **Sales & Marketing** – Any of the "Diplomat" types: Advocate (INFJ), Mediator (INFP), Protagonist (ENFJ), or Campaigner (ENFP)

4. **Human Resources** – Any of the "Extraversion" types: Commander (ENTJ), Debater (ENTP), Executive (ESTJ), Consul (ESFJ), Protagonist (ENFJ), Campaigner (ENFP), Entrepreneur (ESTP), or Entertainer (ESFP)

5. **Technology** – Any of the "Intraversion" types: Architect (INTJ), Logician (INTP), Logistician (ISTJ), Defender (ISFJ), Advocate (INFJ), Mediator (INFP), Virtuoso (ISTP), or Adventurer (ISFP).

6. **Strategy** – Any of the "Explorer" types: Virtuoso (ISTP), Adventurer (ISFP), Entrepreneur (ESTP), or Entertainer (ESFP)

Of course, these are recommendations only and people are more than their personality types. I see these as guidelines for top-level decision making that will need to become more nuanced based on the specific skillset and background of each member of your team.

Once you know what seats to fill, what types of people you'll need, and what personalities go with those seats, you're ready to fill up the bus. Then, as Collins stated, you'll be ready to take that bus somewhere great!

But the bus needs more than the right people and a great destination. You'll need a steady and predictable source of fuel to keep the engine running, and that's where we need to have a conversation about finding the right customers and lining them up like Coke bottles.

The Automatic Exit Framework – Step 6: Line Them Up Like Coke Bottles

Although the Coke bottle we know today was invented in 1915, the shooting gallery is a carnival game that's been played for centuries in hundreds of different ways and under dozens of different names. Ducks in a row, fish in a barrel, stacked milk bottles, or a line of basketball hoops, the game is the same. It essentially consists of putting targets in a row and testing your ability to hit them with a rifle, ball shooter, baseball, squirt gun, you name it.

Now I'm not the most accurate pitcher and I haven't invested the time to become a military-level sharpshooter, but I've found that when they line up the targets in a row like that and just keep them coming, I get pretty accurate. And even inside of a few-minute game, I improve my aim and find I can hit the target more often than not.

That is what we want to create for your marketing that will change how you bring in new clients into your business.

With the first four decisions, you defined how many clients you want to work with. With the fifth decision, you defined your capacity to add clients by deciding who you want on the bus and where you assigned their seat.

Now, let's focus on how you're bringing in clients. The key to lining them up like Coke bottles is to find one method that will consistently bring in as many clients as you want. Everything changes for a business when they have a lineup of new clients coming into the business that are the ideal type of client for them to work with. How do we know if they're the "ideal" or the right client for the business? What do we do about any new or leftover "wrong" clients? I'll talk you through how to solve that problem coming up in Step 7.

For now, let's look at the two biggest problems around clients that I see in small business:

1. Going after too many different types of clients
2. Being overly dependent on too few clients

Looking for Your Coke Bottles

The key to shooting a line of Coke bottles is that they're all the same size and shape. This allows you to build the muscle memory of repeating the same action over and over.

When I first learned to shoot, it wasn't at a carnival game. I was with my dad and older brothers at my grandpa's ranch in Colorado. We started by finding a crate full of old bottles and lining them up along the fence. Then, just as we were getting good at it, but long before we had mastered the skill, we'd pulverized our targets and the game ended to go in search of more bottles we could blast.

This is how most businesses manage their sales process. Too few prospects leaves you with too few at-bats, too few opportunities to master a process and really develop a skill in selling. Instead, your sales process becomes "one-off" or overly custom, and you're left just "figuring it out" with each prospect.

The goal is to have a long line of prospects that look similar and have the same problem for you to solve, and then talk to one right after the other with a similar sales conversation so that you have the greatest opportunity to do business with as many clients as you feel comfortable handling.

Go Where the Coke Bottles Are

The most direct method to line up new prospects like Coke bottles is to go to where there is a supply of Coke bottles already being collected. For our metaphor, that might be a restaurant, a store, or a gas station. Nowadays, all of this glass is recycled, but when I was a kid and we wanted to practice shooting, we just asked the store if we could have some of their bottles and they would hand us six, twelve, or even a case. Today, a kid might have to buy the bottles or arrange a service with the company where he's even charging them a fee for taking away their old bottles.

Let's apply this!

In your industry, there is already someone lining up the empty Coke bottles for you to come and collect. Just find the companies or organizations that already attract or target your ideal customer.

An example would be if you work for business coaches, you might reach out to the organizations that certify or train these professionals and offer to teach their clients something they need that relates to your service. Say, if your company provides lead generation, you could offer a 1-hour course, free-of-cost to their group on how to get new clients. It will provide an added benefit to their customers and will be great for getting you in front of a qualified audience of your own prospects.

Of course, you'll need to make sure your training is *actually* valuable and delivers the result they want, but I've seen that out of a training program like the one in this example, you can always find several businesses willing to hire you to provide your service in place of trying to do it themselves. And I've even seen great synergies where the organization will pay for you to come to their audience and provide your training.

Who is Lining Up Your Clients?

For my white-label digital marketing company, our ideal client was a small to mid-size ad agency that already had a list of clients that needed digital marketing services. So, we went to where they were already collecting our Coke bottles—we joined the local chapter of the American Advertising Federation (AAF or Ad Fed) and began showing up to their events and interacting with other agency owners. This created very organic relationships that led to some of our best and favorite new customers.

One client wanted to reach small business owners in his immediate geographic region, so we set him up with a local small business advisory group where he offered to put free business tips into their monthly newsletter. He was able to simply repurpose content he was creating anyway, send it to them each month, and boom, his company had instant recognition as trusted experts to an entire group of prospects.

More examples?

A high school-age entrepreneur in my town was running a successful but small lawn mowing service and wanted to grow, but he didn't have the skills or money to develop a brand name. Instead, I helped him identify a company that already had the reputation he wanted in a nearby area. He took testimonials from his current customer list and went to the larger landscaping company and said, "I would love to use your name and reputation and I'll work outside of your area and give you a cut of what we're earning." They ended up providing him with the sales training and marketing materials to grow his business and the only cost was a small percentage of the customers *they* helped him bring on!

You sell a system that helps parents get their kids into top colleges. Look at your process and find partners that are going to benefit from your expertise. One of the things a college applicant will need are top test scores, so you could partner with a college test prep company that is already talking to parents that would need your system. Offer them a short video training that they can send out to their list that will help their customers and prospects while simultaneously introducing you to their audience of potential buyers.

Right Person, Right Message, Right Time

With the right philosophy and a clear understanding of your customer, you're ready to activate the best marketing machine in the world. The key to this part of your business is, again, to make it automatic—build it once, turn it on, then set it and forget it!

If you found a way to find your ideal customer, be it through a partnership with the people, a company, organization, software provider, or influencer, find a way to stay in front of that audience with multiple touchpoints, across multiple channels, over a long period of time.

The most difficult part of the old marketing adage to put the "right message in front of the right person at the right time" is actually finding the right person! So, if you've gone through these exercises and done the mental heavy-lifting to determine who your ideal customer is and where to find them, then what's left is simply to know what message they need to hear and then to *keep telling it to them* until they are ready to buy!

The biggest gap our data shows in most marketing campaigns is that the seller gives up too soon on the customer. Many potential buyers, especially in the service industry, are not going to make a purchase decision on the seller's timeline. They will buy when they are in need of the solution, particularly for a complex or sophisticated purchase. So, the job of good marketing is to stay on their radar so that when the buyer is ready to move forward, your company is still top-of-mind in their consideration set.

After you've identified your prospect and made the initial outreach, there are many ways to maintain that awareness. The best way we're seeing companies stay on their prospects' radar right now is through consistent email outreach and ongoing, strategic follow-up campaigns. This is not rocket science, but we consistently see companies that have no follow-up strategy, no CRM or prospect database, and no "set it and forget it" nurture sequence to keep their name and message in front of their hard-earned prospect list.

I can't stress enough how important the follow-up process is for maintaining a new customer pipeline. I'll share more on how my companies have done this when I dive back into my story in Part 3.

Find Influencer Partnerships

Any place where you find someone already talking to

your potential customers, find a way to partner with them to provide value and get introduced to their audience. This will typically be by running a training where you teach some or all of your service, or a workshop or demo of how you would do it for them.

Don't know what they need or what value you can provide? Join the group and ask what they or their clients struggle with. When they tell you, you just have to be ready to say, "Oh, I can help with that. Let's put together a free training that gives value to the group" and then ensure that everyone you present to sees you as the instant authority.

Find the people, organizations, or software that already reaches your audience and find out how you can help them. Then, line up their customers to become your next customers and start knocking them down like a line of Coke bottles on a fence. Likes shooting ducks in a row, you and your team will get better if you're able to simply rinse and repeat the same steps to turn similar prospects into new customers with similar buying journeys. Then, with enough new customers lining up to work with you, you have the enviable problem of deciding which of those customers you want to work with and which of them you want to fire.

The Automatic Exit Framework – Step 7: Fire Your Clients

It will seem counterintuitive at this point, after so much emphasis on deciding who you want to serve as your ideal client, then building a system for lining up all those new prospects and doing the work to convert them into clients, to then tell you the next crucial step is to learn how to fire your clients, but this is an absolute gamechanger in the growth of your business.

In step 1, you redefined your audience down to only include the types of people and companies you love to work with. From this point forward, I challenge you to refuse to work for anything or anyone less than your favorite client.

Just don't do it!

If they aren't a good fit for you going forward? Fire them.

If they don't value the work you're doing? Fire them.

If they don't respect you or the members of your team? Fire them.

You've got to set these boundaries and stick to them relentlessly. Now that you've transformed your role from being a business owner to a business seller, this is now one of your most important jobs: finding the right clients and firing the wrong clients.

Why do You Have Bad Clients?

From our experience, new businesses will take on many (or even most) of their initial clients out of necessity. "They had a credit card and a pulse" is often the criteria cited for new customers at the start of the business. But you're past that point now.

Can we agree that not all clients are created equal? Some

are good—they reply to your emails, they answer your phone calls, they approve creative within one or two rounds of revisions. That's nice, right? They're not all dream clients but that's a pretty good client right there and we want those. We fight to keep those.

Then, there are the other clients—the ones who always seem to be pushing you past deadlines, making everything last minute, ones who call or text after regular business hours, who send you emails right as you're trying to leave for lunch or out the door on vacation. Clients who just consistently are making unreasonable demands of your business.

Now, I'm not going to go into depth on the specifics of why a client might have become a bad client, or on what your own agency might have done to cause that—like they say in pet training: there are no bad dogs, just animals that got stuck with a poorly-trained human.

So, the *cause* of having a client with bad habits is hard to pin down, and there may be blame that can go around. In some cases, it's our industry: they had bad agency experiences before you ever got involved, or they heard stories of shady practices going on at some other shops. Some of that we can't fix, which goes right back to the pet metaphor—it's not your fault the dog's previous owner was lousy, but the poorly-trained dog is now your problem.

Working with a Bad Client

So, define for yourself what a bad client looks like, then, let's define how you're going to work with them.

You should try to work with a client, even a difficult one. In fact, I count on the first two-to-three-months with every new client as a period of getting to know each other, of having some healthy back and forth about deadlines and deliverables. But I am alert for certain deal-breaker behavior. We'll come back to that in a moment.

For the most part, just like dating, you can't go into a client relationship looking for a reason that it's not going to work out, right? I mean, working with people requires that we be patient, flexible, and withhold premature judgment. We're in the service business. Our client is our customer, so providing customer service forces us to make some allowances.

So, the question of when to decide that a client is "bad" is a little bit tricky, and in our determination, one that needs to be handled on a case-by-case basis. Is that fair? Let me give you an example from my own experience.

A Bad Client Example

My agency worked with a client that had a track record of changing agencies every few years. And when this client came to us, the manager—we'll call her Clio, though that's not her real name, of course—but Clio had a large budget. She seemed to know exactly what she wanted from her digital marketing campaign, giving clear direction. And so, we got to work. And after about one month, we met with her and showed her what we'd done, and, we were excited to present because we were doing everything she'd asked.

She was very polite, but she immediately told us that she also wanted several other things done. Does this sound familiar? She hadn't mentioned any of this before, but suddenly, she had more demands: Facebook ads and posts needed to be updated more frequently. We needed to be adding our content to two additional sites. She wanted us to be collecting new leads from new sources, and she had more members of her team that she wanted us to let weigh in for review—classic scope creep, right? The expansion of requested duties after the contract has been signed. And also, she wanted more and more elaborate reporting from us, even with increased frequency.

Again, I'm not bemoaning the situation itself. We all live with the realities of a client-based business. But here's how the next part of the story went:

Now we're two months in, we're still delivering well beyond Clio's initial expectations and the original numbers she gave us. We go into this month's meeting feeling really good about what we had to report. But other signs had begun to creep in, too. Like many clients in the early months, Clio had a tendency to call us with problems, but she tended to call at the very end of the day, or she'd email at like 4:59 on a Friday with a "crisis" for us to fix. These are some pretty baseline signals of a lack of consideration.

So, it's gotten to the fifth month's meeting, we sit down across from Clio, and our team is saying things like, "Hey, when we started, you asked us for 40 leads per week at a cost of $100 per lead. This month, we delivered 80 leads a week and our cost is $60 per lead." So, the team is proud of our results and happy to report the work we've done. We're sitting there, feeling good, and that's when we saw the crazy come out of Clio that maybe she had been hiding in months one and two.

And that's when we finally got why it wasn't the fault of her past agencies that she's been changing vendors every twelve to eighteen months. She says, "Hey, if you guys get me 80 leads this week, I'll want 100 next week. If you get me 100, then I'll want 150. This is just business," she says to my team, "and my job as a client will be to always push you guys to give me better results." And then, to seal the deal, she said, "I'll never be satisfied with the work you do, because I'll always be pushing you guys for more."

So, yeah, when a client actually tells you the words, "I will never be satisfied with the work you're doing for me," that's a good sign that you may need to fire them.

You may have had those moments in your own business, when you're faced with decisions. We work with all types of people. We each bring our own personalities to our business, and we allow clients that same right. But I talked about "deal-breakers" before, and for the good of my company and the respect I had for my team, I told them we wouldn't be continuing our work for her.

Following that last meeting, we formally told the client that we are choosing not to renew their contract, but suggested some other solid agencies that might work well for them. It was a little messy, but at the same time it wasn't, if that makes sense. We finished our work, gave them access to the assets that were contractually theirs, even helped transition their accounts out of our system, and then we never heard from Clio or her team again.

Protect Your People

The good news is, it's rare. I mean, it should be. I choose to believe that most people are innately good, but I've connected with many business owners who have shared the sentiment that you have to protect your company, your reputation, your people, and your own self-respect.

Your team is your company's greatest asset, so ensuring that they have a positive work environment is paramount. Choosing your people over client work or "chasing the money" deepens their loyalty and trust because they know that their leadership has their back.

If it's a one-time or even a short-term problem, address it directly and see if you can move past it. But if not, life is too short to go through your workday dealing with negative, poisonous people who don't respect what you're doing.

The Right Way to Fire a Client

So, you've decided enough is enough, you've given them a chance (or chances), and you're still seeing a long-term pattern of worsening behavior. You know you're better off without them. Is there a right way to cut this cord?

Yes! The good news is that there is a right way to do this. In more than a decade of agency work with hundreds of clients, I have personally developed a system for making the break-up that I can share with you.

#1 – Define a Good and Bad Client

The first, key part to this whole process is really you as an agency—as an ownership or a management team—need to define for yourselves who you do *and do not* want to work with.

At my previous agency, just to share from our particular story, we sat down and talked through this stuff every few months during those early years. These don't have to be hard discussions, but it's valuable to spend the time in leadership meetings to bring up how specific clients are working out for the company and how they're treating your team.

#2 – Communicate with the Client

The second step is to tell the client that it isn't working. In some ways, business has many parallels to other relationship skills, and so this can be compared to going into a breakup.

With your significant other, you may have to have direct moments where there's a "DTR" – a time to stop and "Define the Relationship." In business, there's a moment when you have to be upfront with the client and say, "Hey, stuff's not working for me. Or stuff's not working for you." And then invite them to have a discussion about how things are going to be moving forward

#3 – Offer Them Alternatives

Is there another way forward? Could you freelance this through a member of your team? Could you do this differently for them and avoid the problem?

Depending on the strength of your relationship with the client or your understanding of their needs, step three might be to try to help them transition to a new vendor.

Again, if it makes sense and is possible, offer to give them other ways to fulfill your service or solve that problem for their business.

If you know you're not meant to work with them, it's a mutually beneficial process to help find them a place to go... you know, instead of you.

#4 – Slow Down Your Service

Step four is to actually slow down your service. If you've done the above steps and they are on their way out, or worse, they don't seem to get it, you can reduce the work you're doing for the client, or even just reduce the service you provide, like reporting or phone calls.

Going from bi-weekly reports to monthly, or cutting back to one call a month, will reduce the workload and ease the burden on your team. Who knows? Maybe that will make the client worth working with again.

#5 – Raise Your Price

Step five is to raise your price. In the same vein of reducing the service or frequency, you can make the client more eager to switch vendors by changing the price up.

We did this successfully with several clients at previous agencies where we were even able to actually convince a few of our clients to fire us! It was magic.

A Successful Client Firing

First, as a team, we met together and were very honest about what we did well and what we did not do well for this client. I'll reiterate that this first step is critically important in your preparation for when you get to step two of actually telling the client why you aren't the right agency for them. You have to be convinced so that they will be convinced.

Step three, we came in with a few recommendations for other services that they may or may not want to look into, it's their decision, not ours, but we inarguably made it clear that they should start looking for another agency.

Again, this would not the best way to break up with your significant other, but in the agency world, you really can come across with the highest integrity by conveying that you're looking out for the best interests of the client by stating, "Hey, this isn't working for us, and this probably isn't working for you."

Now, if that works ... you're done! You actually did it in three steps instead of five. Congrats! And there's no rule that you have to go through all five steps.

In some cases, the client is going to get it by the time you're coming in suggesting other places for them to get the work. They may have picked up on it at that point, but in my experience, some clients have proven slow to get the hint. Maybe they resist change for whatever reason, and so, step four is the best and logical next step for their benefit as well as for everyone on your team.

With this particular client, they really had a member of my team jumping through hoops, and everyone on our side agreed we had done our best, even bent over backwards on a few occasions, and still couldn't keep up with their shifting demands.

After we had conveyed steps one through three, we just stopped replying right away to their emails. It felt good for the whole team, and you can imagine the account manager loved when I gave her the assignment to only read that client's emails after lunch. I told her not to worry about them when she came in in the morning—don't even check them!

Also, they had gotten into a habit of texting the account manager when they needed things. So, next I said she could only reply to their texts with the blanket response: "Please email me the details and I'll look into it for you."

And remember, she is only allowed to check those emails after lunch. So, that slowed things way down for her with that client. She was a great account manager, and at first, I think she was anxious about the sudden strategy change until I explained, "Relax, we already know we're going to lose that client." I reminded her we that we'd already met and decided they needed to be gone, and pointed out, "We've really got nothing to lose at this point."

I remember then that for her, and the whole team, it actually became a fun process again because we were being intentional about wanting this client to move on and the last weeks were the best we'd ever had with them!

Which takes me to step five, when you get to start raising the price. Now, you can't just do this all of a sudden, I believe. Or maybe you can—I guess it depends how quickly you're pulling off the band-aid. For us, we typically started on the next call, the one after the "DTR" conversation, by telling them, "Hey, we looked into it the service we've been providing you and it's really more than we had initially expected."

You may notice a lot of my hypothetical conversations begin with the word, "Hey." To me, that conveys that I want these to be casual and sincere, even though the ideas you're going to discuss have been prepared and reviewed beforehand, you need to be there, in the moment, feeling and listening for what the client needs to hear from you.

We go on with the conversation like this: "We're providing more than we had originally planned with your campaign. Of course we're happy to keep providing that service, but we're going to have to right-size our billing." I like using the term "right size" because it is impossible to define, but it gets the point across that "it isn't our fault, it's just not *right*." That makes it easier to get the client to agree with this statement and be on the same side with you when you work with them, saying "we've got to make it right."

I even recommend that you can throw your accounting team under the bus by using a line like, "We looked into it with accounting and they need us to adjust our pricing with you." I mean, it's true, right? They're not necessarily *making* you do this, but, you know, it's not your fault. They're just "right sizing" the account. In our experience, it's less important what you say, but only that you clearly express that a price change is coming.

With this specific client, we had the conversation and said that we'd be adjusting their billing up from where we'd been at six thousand a month, up to seventy-five hundred starting in three months. And that starts the countdown! Again, it's imperative that you're being very upfront with them. You're telling them this is going to change, and you've put a deadline in place and made it clear it's not a bad thing.

Then you get to wait and see what they do.

We've seen more than one client that keeps on like this for another five or six months—until we'd almost doubled what we'd initially billed them! Then, when they finally quit our accounting was like, "Guys, are we sure we want to lose them? They've become a really profitable account for us."

So, that's a good change of pace! It makes you feel like you're back in control.

So, try it for your own business, and if you get all the way to Step Five, you've given them the heads-up that they need to change agencies, that you're not the right fit, and you're telling them the work you're doing for them isn't going to continue the way it's been going, and finally that the price is going up, you should find that they either become the kind of client you want to have, or that they one day just amicably reach out and just let you know they're ready to part ways.

It's truly a win for everyone when it's done effectively, and I can tell you there's no benefit of doing great work for a client that doesn't value you and your service. It's never worth putting your company or your people through that kind of damaging or just draining relationship.

Why Don't We Fire All Our Clients?

So, if it's so good for our business, boosts the morale of the team, and honestly, it just feels good to do it, then why don't we go ahead and fire all of our clients?

Well, besides the fact that you need them for revenue,

the main reason I've found that agencies don't fire their clients, even the difficult, damaging, disrespectful ones that we've talked about that *should* be fired, is because we feel like we can't find better ones.

We feel stuck. Trapped. Isn't a bad client better than no client? One owner termed it this way, "It's difficult to turn down even a lousy meal if it's sitting right in front of me and I don't know where the next hot meal is going to come from." Because the lifeblood of the agency, the source of income and fuel for growth, is having billable clients, we have a hard time telling them no, let alone, letting them go. The answer isn't to fire all of your clients, it's to fire the bad clients and then, keep and add only the good ones.

Now, Add Only Good Clients

You should see now why this step can only come *after* you have a system for getting new clients that you're lining up like Coke bottles. I talk a lot about getting the right message to the right person at the right time. That goes for you, as well, as you're reading this book! At this stage of the Ten Step process, I often reiterate to my client, the business seller, the message that "things tend to get harder before they get better."

It is now your job to hold the line on what a qualified or ideal new customer looks like. You're not desperate. You're no longer in startup mode—taking any client that can pay the bill and "fog a glass." Now, you're building the company that *someone else* will want to buy, and that company needs to be full of the kind of good clients that the new owner will want to have on her or his book of business.

Yes, it's hard, but it won't be your problem for long. Rest assured, busy business owner, you've got other, bigger problems that you'll need to take care of, and they're coming up next!

The Automatic Exit Framework – Step 8: Fire Yourself

Are you ready for some good news?

Finally, here in Step 8, you've reached what all of the aspiring business sellers I've worked with agree is the most important step in the process! This is the journey we set out on from page one of this book, the ten steps for you to make the necessary change from being a business owner to becoming a business seller really culminates at Step 8 when you learn to fire yourself!

The bad news? This is the most difficult step.

Typically, when we consult with business owners who have been inundated for years or even decades with the work of building their business, hiring their team, and taking care of their customers, we often find that the act of separating them back out from the business feels akin to an invasive surgery or having to remove a vital organ—they honestly don't know how they'll function without it!

Stated plainly, the goal of Step 8 is to completely remove you from the functioning of the company. Yes, it's time to get you out of the job and your name entirely off the org chart! Doing this correctly means that there is no part of the day-to-day operation or the customer fulfillment process that relies on you. You are no longer ever allowed to be the linchpin or throttling point on any daily or recurring aspect of the business. Ever!

Getting Rid of Your Job

How do you do that? How do you take the business that was built by you, for you, and all about you, and take "you" out of it? That answer to that question can be as simple as two words:

"It depends."

I know, that answer is a cheat! But, in our client experience, it really all depends on how much you, the owner, fight against the process.

You've come with me this far, so I hope you'll trust me as we take the final step off the ledge of being a business owner and land safely in the rare air of being someone who owns a business that someone else will want to buy.

I've stated before that no one wants to buy your "job."

A business buyer doesn't want the work you do each day and the time you trade to take care of customers and employees. They want the ownership of an efficient business that has the ability to make lots of money (both now and into the future) without requiring all of their time, energy, and attention. So, make *that* your job, the job of leading the company, hands-off, from behind the scenes and completely off the org chart, and you will have a business that someone wants to buy, and more, will pay you a strong multiplier or your top asking price for it!

How Long Can Your Business Run Without You?

Is your business autonomous? How long could it run without you? Two days? Five days? Two weeks? How about two months? Would it seem amazing to you if you could go on vacation for two months and not have to worry about the company you built?

The right answer needs to be "forever." That without you there, in the office, checking on things and making the decisions every day, the company would be just fine to keep running forever.

In fact, in *The Four-hour Work Week*, Tim Ferris says that in his definition of a successfully running company, the owner "could never go to work again and the business would probably run better."

That is the goal we are aiming for. Can your business run better without you? It's another way of asking "what do you do right now for the company that you shouldn't be doing?"

Analyze What You Do

I told you, "It depends." We consistently find that the ease and pace at which you can fire yourself from your job as the business owner depends on how entrenched you are in the company right now.

If you're working full-time, forty or more hours a week, we need to know what you're doing with your time so that we can get you to stop doing it. For those of you with ad agency background or project management training, you may already know what's coming...

You're going to need a time tracker!

At this stage of our consulting, we ask the business owner to track his or her time down to the minute through the next two-to-four weeks to really get granular about their time usage. Longer is better, and we really mean we want every minute of the day so we can know what you're doing with your time.

Do we really need to do this? Yes. We've found that many business owners have no idea how they spend their week, or worse, they *think* they do and are often mistaken. So, we need the real-life, actual data as it happens during the next two-to-four weeks. Just do it for now. You might be surprised at what you learn about how your time is spent!

And yes, you can bring others along on this adventure. We recommend at least leaning on your administrative assistant to help keep track of your time. Or you can keep these results to yourself. We won't judge!

We recommend using a daily planner with spots for at least each half hour, or even each fifteen-minute increment in order to get the actual information on how you're using your time. The customizable time tracker we built for our clients is available here:

www.automaticexit.org/tracker

Use what works for you, but don't skip this exercise!

Do, Delegate, or Delete

Go through the two-to-four-week period and track

what you're doing, writing it down in minute-by-minute increments so you can look back and account for where you spent the greatest portions of your time.

Leading a team meeting for sixty minutes? Write that down. Chatting with an employee about the weekend? Write that down, too. If you do it during the time you have dedicated for work, you should write it down.

What are we looking for? The things you do that you shouldn't be doing. At the end of each day during your tracking period, go back through your schedule and label it as something that is working as a business owner or as a business seller. Or worse—as an employee.

Grab two highlighters: green and pink. We'll refer back to the E-Myth Revisited for our categories:

> **Green:** Working "On" the Business - Highlight everything that only you can do, it cannot be delegated, and it is working on helping to sell the company. This should be your tasks that a business seller would do.
>
> **Pink:** Working "In" the Business - Mark everything that is busy work, that is related to keeping the company running, but could and *SHOULD* be delegated to someone else.

Congrats, You're Fired

The final piece of Step 8: Fire Yourself, is to look at the stuff in pink and decide who should be doing it *instead* of you. Ideally, this could fall to someone already in your organization, typically your COO (or equivalent ops person). In rare cases, you may need to bring on another person to take over these responsibilities. We've solved this through creating titles such as Chief of Staff or the Office of the President if they are temporary roles that won't be required after the sale of the company but make the decision to delegate the work to someone else.

You may have some things on your task list that aren't marked in either color. These may be tasks that you simply delete. We find many business owners have created tasks that are totally unnecessary or that nobody should be doing. You get to decide if you want to keep doing these, but know that the highest and best use of your time will eventually need to become selling the company. Now you're preparing the company to sell, then you'll be finding buyers, interviewing brokers, agents, and answering the mountains of questions that will come next in the selling process.

That's it. You've completed the most difficult step of the ten-step process. From this point on, you shouldn't be coming into work every day with a list of things to do—at least not for your clients! You should only be meeting with your top people or executive team and then making time in your schedule for the ninth step of the Automatic Exit Framework.

The Automatic Exit Framework – Step 9: Set Fire to Everything

A strong psychological shift should be happening for you now in your business. Or rather, it's a shift in the relationship *between* you and your business. Since we started this book, I've challenged you to recalibrate your mindset towards becoming a "business seller" and we've worked together to distinguish how that's different from the typical "business owner" mindset. But it's not until completing Step 8 where, for the first time, as my client business owners truly separate themselves out from the customers, deliverables, and the true day-to-day of their business, I see them start to elevate their sights and really view the big picture of what's going on in the business, and especially how it might be perceived by an outsider.

This is essential for the ninth step, because now is the time when we ask you, from your newly secured vantage point as the business seller, to look at your company objectively and determine what could go, what needs to go, and what absolutely must stay.

We had you fire your clients when they were no longer the right fit.

We had you fire yourself for the same reason.

Now, we're going to make you deconstruct and reconstruct the whole business from the ground up. We call this step: Set Fire to Everything.

What Would You Save?

You've heard the thought exercise, "If your house were on fire, what one thing would you save?" The goal of this question is to create priority and focus. You have to review what you have that is of value and decide to discard or "let go" of everything else.

The most common answer to this scenario has traditionally been family photo albums. That answer has recently changed to be a phone, laptop, computer, or hard drive, as more of our memories are captured digitally. The answer is also often an heirloom or other item of great value. Regardless, when it comes down to this question of permanence and priority, the answer is that we would rescue whatever is irreplaceable to us.

If we were to ask the same question about your company, it should come down to the same things—what's irreplaceable about your business?

Go ahead and take a moment to review your answer for your own business. What is the one thing that, if you had to put your hands on it and hypothetically pull it from the burning building, you would consider to be irreplaceable?

In our experience presenting this exercise to dozens of business owners-turned-business sellers, we find it's not the customers, or the contracts, or even the people in their company—that one's often hard to come to terms with. I mean, of course we value people and can't underestimate the impact they make—and they'd hopefully be able to save themselves from our metaphorical fire—but the irreplaceable part of the company we hear about time and time again is the process of *how you do the work*. The unique systems and standard operating procedures (SOPs) that make up the "how" of your company's business are the part that has the strongest, most irreplaceable value.

Think about it, these are often the closely guarded methods, proprietary processes, even secret formulas for how you do what you do. And most companies have taken years of investment, analysis, trial-and-error, relationship building, and deep-in-the-trenches experience to determine those systems.

Believe me when I tell you, that's the part of the company worth buying. And that's exactly what the next owner, private equity group, or investor is going to want to pay top dollar for. So, how do we determine what those processes are for your business, and, more crucially, how much they are worth?

Your Business is Like a House

Think of your business like a house. Every house shares similar features: four walls, a roof, a bedroom, a kitchen, but how those features work together makes the house unique and special. In our metaphor, that's what makes your business valuable. Every business needs a customer, sales and revenue, operations and fulfillment, but the necessary differences in these requisite features makes your business processes and systems unique and special.

Because when we consult on how to build the business, we use the comparison of building a house, naturally, when we get to our consulting on *selling* the business, we relate this unfamiliar and complex process to the far more familiar activity of selling a house.

Just as you worked hard to build your house until it had the design and furnishings you've come to rely on, the same is true for your business. Even to the point where you may be too close to it to be the best person to determine its value.

For that reason, when you're ready to sell your house, you should turn to experts and professionals to help you price and place the home for sell. Typically, to determine the value of your house, you look at houses comparable in construction, age, square footage, and geography. Those "comps" help you get a general valuation for a similar house. But you will eventually hire a professional to come into your home and provide the estimate for your specific house.

Determining Business Value

This works the same for your business. A buyer or broker will require an estimate in the form of a business valuation by a known and respected valuation company. You may already know that a good business valuation will take into consideration not only the quantifiable things about your company, but the intangibles like your systems, processes, brand, and reputation.

Beyond the typical requirement of five years of financial history (I've seen a bare minimum requirement of three), a solid business valuation should include the following information:

- Gross Margin
- Average Annual Growth Rate
- Percent of Annual Recurring Business
- Client Mix Analysis and Revenue Mix Analysis

- Key Employee Analysis
- Key Risk Analysis

The obvious goal of the valuation is to come away with a reasonable and practicable "selling price" for your business, somewhat akin to a NADA or Kelly Blue Book price for a used car. What I especially like about business valuations that is very unlike a car value is that they are typically communicated in a range. I believe that fairly conveys that although there is a lot of math, modeling, and specific equations applied, this is far from a precise science. With that thinking, I caution clients that a different buyer is going to see a different value and "do different math" to come up with his or her own number.

Any idea that a business has a true or "objective" value is undermined by two illustrations:

1. A homeowner will pay less for a lot to build his or her own home than a developer would pay for the lot to build a multi-family unit, and a business would pay more for the same lot to build a store, not because the lot itself changes value, but because the expected return on the investment is greater.
2. The newspaper boy on the street would never sell his paper for a quarter if it cost him a quarter.

In order to make a sale, the object for sale cannot hold the same value to the seller as to the buyer. One has to value the other thing more than his own thing in order to justify any exchange.

Value is in the Eye of the Beholder

In addition to showing a range of potential price on any valuation, I am also particular about including a timeline for a business value. I again caution clients that a business changes in value not only from buyer to buyer, but from time to time.

The valuation that I prefer to receive for our clients from a respected leader in the marketplace allows for predictive modeling to not only estimate what the business will look like with a three, four, or five-year forecasted value, but that also allows me to toggle various levers inside of the business forecast model to determine what changes will have the greatest impact on the future value.

Back to our example of selling a home, where home estimates show that buyers value some upgrades and renovations more than others, we are able to help business sellers know which investments into the company will yield the greatest increase in total business valuation over time.

It is the equivalent of telling a homeowner that spending ten thousand to tear off and put on a new back deck will not give her the same increase in home value that a ten-thousand-dollar improvement in the kitchen or master bedroom would. I like to run this analysis with a few scenarios for clients to show where they should best spend their time, money, and focus to get the greatest return at the sale of the business. Typically, an investment in sales, marketing automation, or client retention is going to outweigh the returns on investments into secondary business systems, but wouldn't it be valuable to have this specific information for your own company before you invest one minute or one dollar?

Valuations and Predictive Modeling Over Time

For example, here is a valuation and timeline for a company with a current $1.9M valuation. Predictive modeling shows that projecting a 12% increase in sales will have a 25% increase in company value.

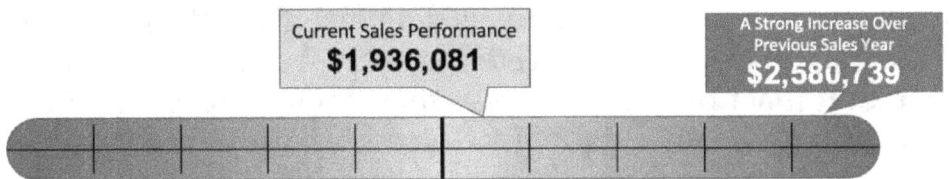

Using the same company, data, and valuation inputs, predictive modeling shows that shifting the company's current client and revenue mix from their higher-risk scenario earning 80% from the top 20% of their clients to a more desirable mix will have a nearly 10% increase in value to the business.

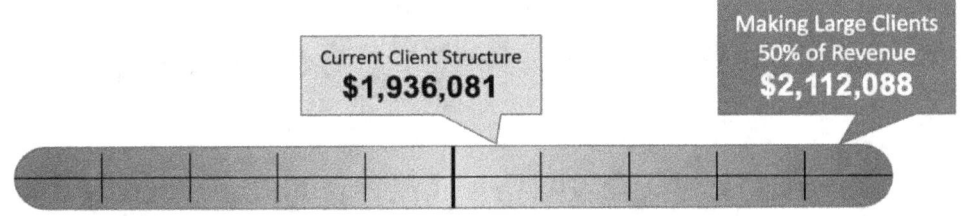

The same predictive modeling for this company shows that even a minor reduction, 10%, from their current operating costs would have a significant impact, 30%, on the future value. This might just be a focus on fewer, larger clients that may not even require any major change in day-to-day operations.

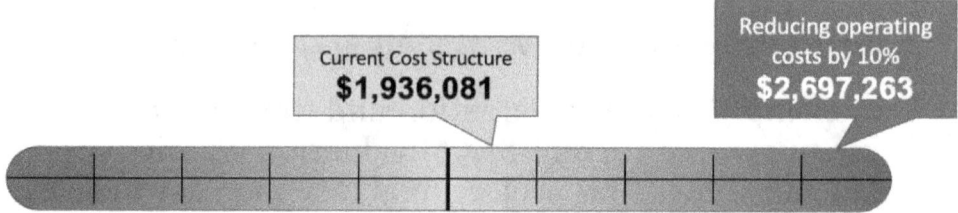

Implementing each of the individual changes above would improve the business's appeal and ultimate sales value. However, predictive modeling reveals that the real impact on value comes when those improvements are applied synergistically. In combination, we see an immediate next-year's enhanced value that more than doubles.

Furthermore, our modeling predicts that if those changes and improvements are extended even just one more year into the future, the value jumps dramatically.

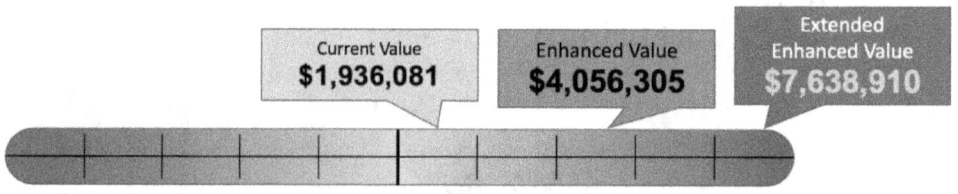

A wholistic valuation with a timeline and predictive modeling of various impacts on the business will create the best starting point for a solid multi-year exit plan. It also gives you actionable data to make an informed decision about what in the business should go, what should stay, what you should invest in, and even the priority of those investments.

From your hard-earned new perspective as a business seller, and with the information from a well-developed valuation informed by predictive modeling and future price forecasting, you're in a much better position to layout your business exit strategy for the greatest success.

By completing the thought exercise of "Setting fire to everything" along with the quantitative exercise of establishing a current business valuation layered with predictive modeling, you will have everything you need to create a reliable three-to-five-year exit plan. And with that, you've completed nine out of the ten steps for an Automatic Exit and transitioning yourself from business owner to becoming a business seller.

You've come so far on this journey, now you just have to stick with the plan, continue down the trail, and cross the final bridge.

The Automatic Exit Framework – Step 10: Now, Cross the Bridge

I grew up in the age of Super Mario Bros. and this game had a formative impact on my life.

Four lessons I learned from Mario are, first, that challenges and setbacks can be seen as a game that we learn from. Second, that when things get too difficult, it's a good idea to save and take a break for a while. I may have learned that one with a bit of help from my mother. Third, I learned the weird lesson that sometimes there are "warp zones" that let you skip over challenges you don't have to face. I'm still learning this one, actually, but I try to take warp zones instead of unnecessary challenges whenever I get the chance.

But, most relevant for Step 10 of the Automatic Exit Framework, I learned that at the end of each level, there is a bridge that must be crossed. If you, too, played more Mario than you should have, you know all about the bridge. While some of you may be wondering if there even was a bridge in that game or where it showed up. It was at the end of each world, at the end of the final level, when you faced the boss. It was always over lava. It was what separated you from the princess you were there to rescue. And it was always protected by a dragon.

The "dragon" in Super Mario Bros. is named Bowser. And what is interesting about Bowser is that, for all his bigger size, spikey body armor, and even the fact he breathes balls of fire, he isn't actually that hard to beat.

If you know how.

If it's been a while for you, I'll pause here to play a few levels of the game (for research) so I can give you a brief and accurate refresher. If my review has suddenly reminded you of the awesomeness that is this video game classic, you might also want to pause here and enjoy a nostalgic revisit to the world of Mario. You know, for research.

Don't Fight the Dragon

Unlike pretty much every other bad guy in the game, Bowser can't be killed by stomping. But that's Mario's main weapon! He runs, jumps, breaks bricks, and stomps. In the rare and special instances when he has a fire flower, he can also shoot fire. But that's it. Those are your options. All of those would mean that Bowser is very hard to kill in a fair fight. Except that Bowser is standing on a bridge.

I look back and think it's funny that the video game designers made it this way. You don't actually "fight" the giant turtle-shelled dragon at the end of the game. You "outsmart" him. Imagine this from the in-game perspective of Mario—you're smaller, weaker, weaponless, and unarmored—not to mention, ostensibly, your only training is as a plumber. What are you doing on a lava bridge facing a big, scary monster of an opponent? The brilliance of this boss battle is that, when every instinct should be telling him to fight for his life, which is ineffective here, or run the other way, the only solution is to face his fear and *run at the enemy!*

It brings to mind Robert Frost's quote on human suffering, "The best way out is always through."

When selling your company, like in Mario, when you come to the final boss, the bridge is the point of decision. To cross or not to cross? You've decided to sell the company means you've chosen to cross the bridge. The deal is the princess, the prize that you're seeking, and it's waiting on the other side. And the dragon, well, the dragon on the bridge is your own fear.

Your fear is not the enemy. Fear is normal. And healthy. Humans come strongly equipped with the desire to avoid the unknown, to stay where you are, and to not have to change or do "the difficult thing." When we're forced into a conflict, our heartrate accelerates, our field of view narrows, and we instinctively choose between a fight, flight, or freeze response.

It's uncomfortable. It's literally the definition of being afraid. And we are here to help our clients do it anyway.

You Haven't Made It This Far Only to Make It This Far

Many of our clients have reached this point in their journey and they're taking a new look at their business, now with the enlightened perspective of someone working *on* the business, not in it, someone actively creating a company that will sell. And from here, they see that things are better now. The company makes more money and demands less of the owner. The management team is handling more, if not all, of the problems that come up each day—problems that used to land on *your* desk! It's easy to get complacent. To avoid the difficult thing. To not want to cross the bridge.

But this is the end of the level! I remind them how far they've come. That they wanted this. That, like death, a company exit is inevitable. Inexorable. And I share this picture of the final boss in Super Mario Bros. and whisper, "Don't fight. Don't flee. Just run at the dragon."

And when they do, they find, that just like in the game, the dragon of their own fears will jump out of the way, they can run right past it, and then you reach the flashing axe that activates the bridge mechanism and drops Bowser into the pool of lava. It's immensely satisfying. And you've beaten the game and saved the princess.

This is your company. Your story. The exciting game of your life. When you feel the stress of making the final decision, or the alluring temptation of complacency after coming this far, face your fear. Cross the bridge. And win the game.

Part 3 – Becoming a Business Seller

Chapter 5: Implementing the Automatic Exit

Okay, my business-selling friend! You've read my story. You've learned the Automatic Exit Framework that has helped hundreds of business owners make the journey. Now it's time for you to walk this path for yourself!

What's stopping you? Hopefully nothing and you are nodding your head and ready to go, already doing the exercises and planning your path to becoming a business seller. But, in my experience, many clients have read my story and learned the framework and then still said, "Now what?"

This is just code for "I don't know where to start." So, in the third and final part of this book, I include a recap and action plan for you, the soon-to-be business seller, to complete and get started. Or, if you've already gotten started, this will get you to the next step. Ready to get motivated? Here we go.

Decide to Decide

As human beings, the hardest thing we do is literally the thing we were designed for: making decisions.

It's true. Of all the creatures on earth, humans are the only ones capable of judgement, **self-analysis,** imagination, abstract thinking, positions of morality, and as far as we can tell, any forms of guilt or regret.

While animals must make certain decisions to survive and reproduce, they are apparently reacting to internal instinct or external environmental stimulation. They demonstrate little "executive control" or conscious consideration about the impact of their decisions on the future or on others.

Humans, on the other hand, make decisions not only with instinct, intuition, or what we call "gut feelings," but with logical reasoning and emotion. In fact, it is our very ability to think abstractly, to envision into the future, and to see the potential consequences of our decisions that create indecision or hesitation.

In my work with over two-hundred small to mid-size business owners, the biggest obstacle isn't that owners don't *know* they need to make a decision, but that they simply aren't making it.

Analysis Paralysis

When we are faced with a decision, even one we know we need to make, we can become overwhelmed or spiral into overthinking the choices ahead of us. This is called "analysis paralysis" and occurs as a state of confusion, heightened anxiety, indecision, and downward-spiraling deliberation on past events, worst-case scenarios, and potential future outcomes.

Except in rare cases of mental health issues such as diagnosable depression or anxiety, most instances of analysis paralysis are manifestations of fear and imagined stress. Psychologist Barry Schwartz summarizes simply in his research entitled the "Paradox of Choice" that having more options will lead to greater anxiety and indecision.

Don't let the amount of options paralyze you. In the case of selling your company, the path is simpler than you might think. The most important thing is to remember that you've already built something of value. You've done the hardest part. Now, you just need to make one clear, proven decision at a time that will take you down the 10-step plan to turn your valuable service company into a sellable asset.

What Decisions are the Most Important?

Not all decisions are created equal. Steve Jobs was famous for wearing the same outfit every day: Levi's 501® blue jeans and a black Miyake mock turtleneck. Taking a page from his book, Mark Zuckerburg is also always seen wearing the same outfit: blue jeans, a gray t-shirt, and hoodie.

Both multi-billionaires state that they adapted this approach to their daily wardrobe because it limited decision fatigue. Essentially, the fewer choices you have to make, the more mental energy you have for making the other, more significant decisions that you'll have to make about your life and work.

In the book *Designing Your Life* by Bill Burnett and Dave Evans, they propose that there are several decisions that fall into the category of being the most significant:

- **Lifeview:** What is your life philosophy? What is the meaning of your life?
- **Workview:** What is the purpose of work? How does your work relate to society and the individual?
- **Current situation:** How are your health, work, love, and play? Where would you like them to be?
- **Imagining the future:** What kind of life would you like to have down the road?

It shouldn't surprise you at this point to learn that I consider the building and selling of your business to be among the most significant decisions of your life. And I believe you have everything you need *right now* to make those decisions and start down the path ... and more importantly, to succeed in becoming a business seller.

The Socratic Method

The ancient philosopher Socrates taught that we already have the answers. I've found it to be true. The Socratic Method is a form of argumentative dialogue that progresses by posing thought-provoking questions that actively engage your analytical and future-thinking abilities to formulate the right answers for your own life.

I encourage you to take the time right now to ask those questions, to decide on your own answers, and to re-decide that you will make the hard decisions, stick to those choices, and become the business seller that can look back and feel content about the life you've lived.

Decide to Re-decide

In certain respects, the 10 Steps of the Automatic Exit Framework are really just three decisions that you have to re-decide about your business.

As we've discussed, you've already succeeded by building a business that has value. The second part of this book was simply asking you to analyze what got you to this point and decide what stays and what goes as you move into the exit planning and "selling" stage of the company.

In groups of three (and one group of four), the 10 Steps are asking you to redefine and redecide *what* you do, *how* you do it, and *why* you're doing it. Let's examine the 10 Steps further by answering these questions for yourself about your business:

REDECIDE WHAT YOU DO

Step 1: Decide who you serve.
Redefine Your Audience. Start with "Who do you LOVE to serve?"

Step 2: Solve the biggest problem.
Redefine Your Offer. What do they need most? How much would they pay for that problem to be solved?

Step 3: Be the best in the world.
Redefine Your Service. What do you need to change to elevate your service to world-class?

REDECIDE HOW YOU DO IT

Step 4: Make it McDonald's.
Redesign Your Fulfillment. How do you create a consistent, reliable, deliverable without *you* doing the work?

Step 5: Assign Seats.
Redesign Your Team. What needs to be done and, most important, *who* will do it?

Step 6: Line them up like Coke bottles
Redesign Your Marketing. How will you create a marketing system where your ideal clients come to you?

REDECIDE WHY YOU'RE DOING IT

> **Step 7: Fire Your Clients.**
> **Redesign Your Client List.** Will you refuse to work for anything less than your favorite clients?
>
> **Step 8: Fire Yourself.**
> **Redesign Your Own Role.** What would your business look like if you no longer worked there?
>
> **Step 9: Set fire to everything.**
> **Redesign the Business to Be "Sellable."** Do you have the roadmap to your most profitable exit option?
>
> **Step 10: Now, Cross the Bridge.**
> **Decide who and how you sell the business.** Can you be fearless, unemotional, and decisive through to the end?

What Do You Do Now?

Alright, you're done! Did you think it would end this way? To paraphrase Gandalf from *Return of the King*, the end is never really the end. No, the journey doesn't end here. But the next path is a new path to a new place. And you should start it with a new answer to a new question.

You already answered that you wanted to become a business seller. And you walked the path to become that person. Now you get to ask the question, "What do you want to become next?" And the answer can be anything you want. In fact, I'm going to be almost zero help with this because it's a personal journey and everyone's answer will differ.

I can't tell you what to become next, but, as before, I believe I can help you by sharing what I did when I faced this choice and hope that allows you to learn any lessons from my personal journey that apply to your own life and future goals.

It's a Personal Choice

After the sale of my company, I took three months off and just relaxed. Mostly because people told me to. And you will probably have many people that say, "You worked so hard, you deserve a break." Or "Why don't you just take some time for yourself." It's well intentioned, but, like everything else, I believe this is a personal choice.

For me, I decided to travel with my family. My kids were nine, six, and four and we rented an RV and drove all over Southern Utah as well as taking a couple vacations to California and Florida. It was amazing, but it was also very temporary, and we all felt that way, which I think helped us appreciate all that "down time" for what it was.

I soon found myself missing work, needing a project or problem to solve, and inexplicably getting into conversations with friends and connections that evolved into talking through business ideas or solving business problems.

It felt almost inevitable when a friend of a friend put me in touch with someone, a former client, actually, who was looking for a consultant to help in the early-stage growth of his digital marketing agency, and I moved back into the familiar work-life balance of having a job, but this time as a freelance (read "1099") consultant. I enjoyed the work and loved the autonomy and personal freedom that came from being neither an employee nor the business owner. It wasn't long, about 8-10 months post-sale, before I turned to my wife and said, "I know what I want to do next!"

The whole truth is that I mostly knew what I *didn't* want to do next, and that was start another agency. I felt no pull to go on the rounds of new client selling, employee hiring and training, and then falling back into managing a team of twenty-year-olds. No thanks. I'd crossed that bridge and was only a little surprised to find I was glad to have it behind me.

Teaching Owners About Ownership

I told my wife I wanted to start a new company, and she patiently waited while I explained that this time it would be a small consulting firm built specifically to help business owners grow, scale, and sell their companies. I knew I'd loved my time as an adjunct professor, getting to teach the things I knew and was passionate about, but unlike teaching a required marketing class to undergrads, this time I'd be teaching the most receptive and energized students possible, people who *actually wanted to know what I knew* because they were about to go through the experience I'd just had. And I knew I wanted to keep it small. Just a few key players and support staff.

I even knew I didn't want a lot of clients. In fact, I believed I could do my best work with just a few, and I knew right where to find them, my own network of agency owners that I'd developed during my years working in agencies and then selling to agencies.

I also knew we could work from anywhere—I'd become location independent—and we discussed where we wanted to "be from" and raise our family. Ultimately, I ended up moving to North Carolina, establishing my consulting company, and telling lots of clients the story I share in this book. But one of the topics I found myself coming back to, as many of my clients are already wealthy and have lived comfortable lives, is *the step that comes after* the last step of the 10 Step Automatic Exit Framework.

The 11th Step

After you have sold your company, life will go on. Don't be so surprised! The message I often end up sharing in discussions with people who find they have "enough" is the encouragement to give back. Giving back can be one of the greatest sources of joy you will ever experience. At this point, you've worked hard and accomplished the kind of huge life goal that many people strive for and few ever achieve. You are comfortable and perhaps even independently wealthy. Now, I would encourage you to be generous to everyone. Especially yourself.

But you will *be* yourself, and by extension, have to live with yourself, for many years into the future. What do you plan to do with your time now? And also with your resources, your energy, the amount of very significant experience that you have amassed? Now that you're a business seller, you have to become the owner of something much more important: the rest of your life!

In his book *Be Your Future Self Now*, Dr. Benjamin Hardy shares the research that reveals this truth:

"As a species, we haven't evolved to plan twenty years into the future."

Have you found that true in your own life? In my consulting, it's a challenge to keep clients focused on five-year or even three-year exit plans. In my personal life, I struggle to plan my own daily To Do list. But what we can do, just as I challenged you to do at the beginning of this book, yes, all the way back in the Introduction (you're not one of those people who reads a book and skips the introduction, are you?) is to decide not what you do, but the person you want to become.

You chose to become a "business seller" and it put you on the path to eventually being someone who *has sold* the business you built. Now, as "someone who has sold a business," I challenge you to become a person who gives more than they take. Be a person who gives back.

The Automatic Exit Framework – Bonus Step: Give Back.

One of the most horrible statistics ever shared with me was the number of wealthy people who are unhappy. In research from 1984 by Deiner, Horwitz, and Emmons at

UC-Davis, they report that 37% of wealthy individuals report being less happy than the average person. (Ed Diener*, Jeff Horwitz and Robert A. Emmons "Happiness Of The Very Wealthy.") Stated differently, more than one-third of "very wealthy" people weren't happy.

This was hard for me to understand because, like so many others, I grew up with the belief that the answer to most problems was having more money. I believed, then that by extension, more money would make people happy. But over and over, the research doesn't bear that out. Statistically, money doesn't make people happy.

So what does? The research tells us that the happiest people are those that live their life with purpose. People that have a cause or a belief that they live in support of. That's what I mean when I tell my friends and clients to give back.

Giving back can be done in so many ways that it really is up to you how and when, where and how often, you decide to do it. For many, it's financial—donating money to organizations and causes they believe in. For others, it's time—in-person serving in your areas of expertise on boards or committees, or even with your own two hands, rolling up your sleeves and digging into community service projects or neighborhood cleanups. For others, it's religious—in the form of paying tithing, other offerings, or funding programs that lift the poor in spirit. Serving missions or going on service trips to help those in need. For others, it's through education—teaching, training, volunteering, or writing blogs, books, and articles about what they've learned.

It can be any or all of these, or something specific to you, but give of your time, your resources, and your expertise to help those around you, especially those that are following behind you and might be looking for an example or mentor of the life they're trying to figure out for themselves.

It's Not What You Make But What You Keep

At some point, my goal changed from how much money I earned to how much money I had in the bank, investments, and how much I would have in the future that I could rely on. Wealth became defined by how much money I *saved*.

Morgan Housel states in his book *The Psychology of Money* that "saving money is the gap between your ego and your income, and wealth is what you don't see."

It's the purchases that aren't made, the new cars that aren't bought, or the new wardrobe not being constantly updated that amounts to the accumulation of wealth. Some of the richest *looking* people you see are actually broke or in debt. Pursuing the appearance of wealth is one of the fastest ways to lose it.

"Manage your money so you can sleep at night. The foundation of 'Does this help me sleep at night?' is the best universal guidepost for all financial decisions."

    –from *The Psychology of Money* by Morgan Housel

I would quote to you the whole book, it's one of the best reads I can recommend on the topic of money, but for copyright reasons, I'll be content with sharing this gem that should become your financial goal:

"The ability to do what you want, when you want, with who you want, for as long as you want to, pays the highest dividend that exists in finance."

"Being able to wake up one morning and change what you're doing on your terms whenever you're ready seems like the grandmother of all financial goals.

Independence to me doesn't mean you'll stop working. It means you only do the work you like, with people you like, at the times you want for as long as you want."

You've earned that kind of independence. You deserve that kind of life. Now, you're in the unique place where you can give back and help others find what you've found.

Chapter 6: My Story and Your Story

Looking back, I wish I'd understood how much of the sale happens before "the sale." There's so much you can impact about the business that will make a difference if you're looking down the road ahead.

Obviously, a buyer is going to want to know how much your company is worth through a valuation. They'll want to see financials. Get a professional valuation—potential buyers are going to expect it, and it'll give you a solid, realistic basis for the price you're looking to achieve.

Prepare a comprehensive packet of financials, with clear profit and loss statements, tax returns, and any documentation that shows a stable, successful business. This packet is your business's "story" in numbers. If there are any upgrades or small investments that could increase the value, make those changes early so they're reflected in the numbers.

But you can get this information so much earlier in the process and there are so many options available for what you can do to make it worth more. With each aspect of the valuation, there are levers you can pull and with proven forecasting models, you can project your valuation based on each of these potential scenarios.

Once you know your numbers, consider how you want to sell. A broker can help list and market your business, but if you want to take a more hands-on approach, you can bypass the broker route and do some research on listing platforms where business buyers are actively looking.

Going without a broker means more direct work but potentially more control over the process and cost savings. Whichever route you take, try to line up more than one potential buyer from the start; having multiple interested parties will give you leverage.

When you're in the early stages with buyers, it's important to maintain a sense of controlled competition. Allow interested buyers to review your financial packet and encourage them to make offers, but keep them aware that others are also interested. It's a bit like running an auction—ask each buyer to give you their best offer by a specific date. This deadline will help you quickly see who's serious and who values your business the most. From there, pick the top three to five offers to move forward with.

As things start to get more serious, stay open and proactive in your communications, sharing information as transparently as you're comfortable with. This isn't the time to be guarded or defensive; buyers are not just evaluating the financials, they're evaluating you as an owner and potential partner in this transaction. Don't let familiarity soften your perspective—they're not your "friends" here, even if they're friendly. They're vetting you as much as you're vetting them. The impression you make will affect how they see the value of your business, its systems, its people, and its potential.

Remember that evaluating buyers is as important as selling them on the business. If you're talking to an individual buyer, understand that they're on a journey, too—from business searcher to business buyer to, finally, business owner. Just as you're moving from owner to seller, they're imagining themselves in your shoes. Have empathy for that transition and consider it in your approach. The best deal is one that meets both of your needs and makes each of you feel confident about the future.

Finally, when you've selected the right buyer, work closely to bring everything across the finish line. Address any final questions they have and be sure your legal and financial advisors are fully engaged to guide you both through the paperwork and the details. It's not just a sale; it's a handoff, and with the right approach, it can be a mutually beneficial transition into the next chapter of life for both of you.

I have been asked if it was hard to sell my company. And when they ask that, they mean emotionally hard, as in was it difficult to separate myself from the business that I'd built and let someone else come in and buy it, take it over, and no longer own the business myself. I've even had it asked and compared to selling one of my children. I tend to compare it more to say, selling a piece of furniture that I made in my garage. And it's like I built a couch, but I'm highly aware of the flaws of the 2 I built and that it's not totally straight or that some of the screws weren't tightened in all the way. And then someone comes along and they're excited about the couch I built and even like, I'll pay you more than you think it's worth to buy that couch from you. And I'm proud of it, but I'm also like, I could build another one of these if I wanted to. And do even a better job of it next time around.

Here's the 6-step Automatic Exit Action Plan

The Automatic Exit strategy is all about getting the most value back you're your most valuable asset. The process will require smart strategic planning, direct outreach, and professional assistance in legal and financial areas.

Step 1. Prepare the Business for Sale
- **Financial Documentation:** Organize detailed financial statements, tax returns, and profit and loss records. A potential buyer will want to see a strong financial history.
- **Operational Documentation:** Document standard operating procedures (SOPs), staff roles, and other key operational aspects to make the business attractive and accessible for potential buyers.
- **Legal Compliance:** Ensure all contracts, intellectual property, licenses, and legal agreements are in order.

Step 2. Determine the Business's Valuation
- Hire a business valuation expert or an accountant to help establish a realistic price range. A third-party valuation will add credibility, even without a broker.

Step 3. Identify Potential Buyers
- **Networking:** Utilize your network to find qualified buyers, such as competitors, suppliers, or former business associates.
- **Direct Outreach:** Create a list of strategic buyers or companies within your industry that may be interested in acquiring your business.
- **Online Platforms:** Use reputable online marketplaces (like BizBuySell, Axial, or DealStream) where you can directly list your business for sale. Note that these are not endorsements. This field is evolving and you'll need to research to find your best current options.

Step 4. Confidentiality and Pre-Qualification
- **Non-Disclosure Agreements (NDAs):** Before sharing sensitive information, require interested parties to sign NDAs.
- **Buyer Screening:** Pre-qualify potential buyers by assessing their financial capacity, experience, and genuine interest.

Step 5. Negotiate and Structure the Deal
- **Negotiation Strategy:** Decide upfront on the terms you're willing to negotiate, such as payment structure, transition support, or seller financing.
- **Legal and Financial Advisors:** While not using a broker, you should still involve an experienced lawyer and accountant to help with the sales agreement, tax implications, and legal compliance.

Step 6. Close the Sale
- Draft a purchase agreement and work with both parties to finalize terms.
- Address regulatory or legal obligations and work with a legal professional to complete the transaction.

Conclusion

Spoiler Alert: Rather or not business owners think they'll ever sell their business, I believe everybody should be building a business they could sell.

It should come as no surprise at the end of this book that my answer to "What kind of business should I build that creates financial and time freedom for myself?" is one that is run with multiple people and systems that allow you to get out of the trap of trading time for money.

The act of transforming your service business into a sellable asset requires you to convert it from "a job someone does" into "a need that your company fulfills."

At my agency, we had a team that delivered the "fulfilled products" we sold. We had productized content, productized SEO and social media ads. We turned each thing that we knew the client needed into one thing that we could package up, develop a process around, and consistently deliver.

Again, there's no employee at McDonald's who stops cooking french fries to go broil a filet mignon, no matter what price you try to pay them.

When you know the audience you're going to serve, you also know (or come to know) the services they're going to need. And you're going to spend a lot of time with this audience, so please, I implore you to pick an audience you care about enough to spend 10 to 40 plus hours a week with talking to and dealing with and thinking about them and their businesses and their customers and their problems. It's unpopular to use the

"L" word in business, but I can attest to the fact that if you work with the type of clients you love, the other aspects of business become that much easier and more enjoyable.

The End—and the Plot Twist

At the beginning of this book, I talked about the powers of good storytelling. I shared what I've learned, that a good book has a good plot twist. Throughout this book, I've referred to your business as your #1 asset—and it is! It's where you've sunk the majority of your worries, energy, time and money.

But time *is* money.

And what is your worry, your attention, focus and energy, your very life, but the allocation of your time? Therefore, time—the hours and minutes that make up your life—is your most valuable resource. The #1 asset that you need to be earning a worthwhile return on is your own life and the investment of your time.

With any investment, you hope to get back more than you put in. Now I'd like to tell you the rest of the story of my own first exit and how I got what I now call an infinite return back on what I had put in.

You see, it's hard to learn the lesson of "How to sell an agency business" from someone who got lucky, hired the right broker, stumbled across their ideal buyer, or otherwise let the process happen to them as easily as stepping off the edge of the diving board to splash effortlessly into a life of luxurious mojito sipping on private beaches.

That person has nothing to teach you because they never learned anything. It was effortless for them, so their counsel would be the trite advice to find the right buyer, broker, and price for your business.

It's the same reason Einstein would be a lousy math tutor. The work was too easy for him, and teaching it is not his skill. "You just do it!" or "It's not that hard" is terrible consulting for someone struggling to learn a new concept.

My exit was not a leisure dive into an awaiting blue pool. It was more of a barreling waterslide ending with an ice-cold splash in the face.

Because of the way my contract was written, in the legalese supplied by our "company lawyer" who was the brother of the president, my ownership percentage was never activated.

When we sold the company I'd helped build, brand, position, grow, and exit, I got nothing beyond a standard severance. In fact, following an invite-only lunch meeting with the buyers, the president returned to let me know I wasn't among the staff being retained through the transition. And four hours later, I was jobless and holding my final paycheck on a Tuesday after being told to take the rest of the week off.

So, I didn't learn how to exit a company with a golden parachute on my back and a cool drink in my hand. I like to say I learned how NOT to exit, how not to trust blindly in a partner, broker, friend, or legal document, but how to check every detail, ask the hard questions, and turn over every uncomfortable rock.

I learned the painful lesson of doing the deal badly for myself so that I can now be in the best position to see the potholes and pitfalls in my clients' paths to selling their own agencies.

The Most Important Step

When we decided to sell, we tried to do it on our own first and basically spun out for three plus months. Then, someone heard our problem and said they knew a guy who had sold his business to Infusionsoft for millions of dollars and said we should talk to him. So, we got them to set up time with him. And it turned out he'd sold a different type of business to a totally different buyer from what we were looking at, and he didn't have relevant advice for us, and he didn't really have a way to help with what we were doing, but we talked him into being our business selling coach and he magnanimously agreed to give it a try with us for the upfront sum of sixty-thousand dollars and then six percent of the sales price in the eventual liquidity event, which is about the same as what you pay the broker who does the actual deal for you.

So, we end up paying this guy we'll call "Rusty" about $60,000 for about six months of work, which may have actually been about six hours of work looking back at what he actually did for us, which was meeting for a few lunches and telling his story a few different times, and then making a small handful of intros.

And it was frustrating because we still walked about every step of the way on our own and when we finally found a few buyers, our anxiousness and uncertainty let us rush the process and we did the whole deal too fast and for too little money, and ultimately, perhaps to the wrong buyer.

Now it's Your Turn

Looking back, the most important step was deciding that we wanted to sell our company. Then, I would say, the next most important step was deciding how we wanted to sell it. But we were left on our own for this part.

My advice is, once you've made the decision to sell, and you've got in mind your current value and your exit number, the goal price you want to reach to finally sell your hard-earned asset for, you don't decide how you're going to do every little step.

You can't know it all, you can't plan it. You can't map from the outset how it is all going to go in your specific case. But you can decide who you'll get for your guide. Decide who knows how to get where you're trying to go, and who's walked that exact path before. A dozen times. A hundred times. Decide who can help you do it and you're already halfway there. Decide what you want, then find the advisor, the mentor, the coach and guide who's already been where you're trying to go and knows the way. And then, just copy what they did. Get them to show you how they did it.

If you want to sell an agency like yours for millions of dollars, find someone who's done it and say, "Show me how you did that." Better yet—ask them to do it with you. Guaranteed success, right? You don't know what's coming next, but a good mentor absolutely does, and with them, now you're not a novice walking this path for the first time. You're an expert, too.

About the Author

Shawn Butler is an author, teacher, marketer, entrepreneur, and consultant. He was born in Seattle, went to high school in the Atlanta suburb of Peachtree City, and has lived and studied in Georgia, Utah, North Carolina, and across four continents while learning to speak five and a half languages and earning multiple degrees, recognitions, and certifications in education, training, and leadership.

Shawn holds a BA in marketing from Brigham Young University, an MS from the Sorbonne, and an MBA from Georgia State University. He has taught entrepreneurship, business strategy, marketing and value creation at multiple companies, colleges and universities and is passionate about sharing these concepts with students and business leaders.

Shawn has been part of the successful exit planning and value creation of more than two-hundred small to medium size businesses in the B2B service industry.

You can reach Shawn to learn more about his work and consulting service at shawn@relevant4agencies.com. For more information on this book, visit automaticexit.org.

Appendix - 16 Personality Types

Analysts

INTJ – Architect: Imaginative and strategic thinkers, with a plan for everything.

INTP – Logician: Innovative inventors with an unquenchable thirst for knowledge.

ENTJ – Commander: Bold, imaginative and strong-willed leaders, always finding a way – or making one.

ENTP – Debater: Smart and curious thinkers who cannot resist an intellectual challenge.

Diplomats

INFJ – Advocate: Quiet and mystical, yet very inspiring and tireless idealists.

INFP – Mediator: Poetic, kind and altruistic people, always eager to help a good cause.

ENFJ – Protagonist: Charismatic and inspiring leaders, able to mesmerize their listeners.

ENFP – Campaigner: Enthusiastic, creative and sociable free spirits, who can always find a reason to smile.

Sentinels

ISTJ – Logistician: Practical and fact-minded individuals, whose reliability cannot be doubted.

ISFJ – Defender: Very dedicated and warm protectors, always ready to defend their loved ones.

ESTJ – Executive: Excellent administrators, unsurpassed at managing things – or people.

ESFJ – Consul: Extraordinarily caring, social and popular people, always eager to help.

Explorers
ISTP – Virtuoso: Bold and practical experimenters, masters of all kinds of tools.

ISFP – Adventurer: Flexible and charming artists, always ready to explore and experience something new.

ESTP – Entrepreneur: Smart, energetic and very perceptive people, who truly enjoy living on the edge.

ESFP – Entertainer: Spontaneous, energetic and enthusiastic people – life is never boring around them.

An Interview with the Author by Laura Noland

What is the difference between what you teach and what a business owner can typically find when they're looking at exiting their business?

On my podcast TODAY'S AGENCY, I ask business owners two questions that really convey my philosophy about business ownership. First, I ask them, "What was happening in the business when you hired your first employee?" Because this tells us so much about the mindset of the business owner. Were they always entrepreneurial, did they build this thing from the outset to run without them and to be able to grow?

Well, most agency people are practitioners. They didn't set out to build a company, they set out to take care of a client or to deliver a really good copywriting service or ad management service. That's the danger of a service business: it's focused on the service it provides or on the customer that it's serving and spends its efforts trying to be the best at those services while meeting the needs of those specific clients.

The second question I ask is, "When did you go from 'trading hours for dollars' to really building up a business?" And I could use these questions interchangeably because so often, in the path of the business owner, they're the same thing. The answer to one is the answer to the other. The freelancer, the exhausted one-man-show or solopreneur became the owner of his or her business when they hired their first person and really, at least mentally, began to uncouple themselves and their time from delivering all of the work for the business.

How does an owner know if they are building a business they can exit?

When I talk to agency owners who want to sell their business, of course I need to know what their current revenue, team size, and target audience are. Benchmarking a snapshot of the business as it is today is critical in the initial steps of creating a business valuation. But the more important data, and the most interesting story, is what they were doing before. How they started out and what they originally built tells us the journey they went on to become who they are and to build what they built.

The story I really want to get from the people I'm interviewing is not where you are today: "I have a two million dollars a year business. It has this many employees..." You told me all that in the pre-interview, now I want to hear, "How did you get there? How long did it take? What happened to get you to this point from where you started out?" This is what I'm interested in.

The questions in that interview include asking, "How many days could you be away from the business?" Or "Do you feel like your business could run without you?" I'm trying to narrow down how autonomous the business is.

In the book *The 4-hour Work Week*, author Tim Ferris states, "I could never go to work again and the business would probably run better." That situation arrives only because he has empowered the people who sell the product, he's empowered the manufacturing process, and he's created this business where he's not on the org chart. So, I want to hear that when I talk to business owners. How did they get to that point? How can other business owners follow their example?

Trading hours for dollars is bad. Trading hours for dollars is like the epitome of *not* owning a business. That's being a freelancer—no ability to scale, no more hours in the day, no ability to take on more work—and being a freelancer is bad if you're trying to build a business.

What is the number one mistake that business owners make when they're starting their business?

Honestly, the number one mistake I see business owners make is people doing something they love and turning that into their business. They go to work because they are good at something. And that's dangerous. Whether you're making cabinets, baking cakes, or creating websites, if you love doing the work, you're going to turn yourself into a glorified freelancer. You're going to spend your time and your hours doing that work, which forces you into a model of trading your hours for dollars.

How did you change that mindset, then, from being a "glorified freelancer" to building a sellable business? What are some actionable steps to make that switch?

Well, there's two ways to go from there. And again, the power of that question is you're saying, "How do you go from that to something else?" The next question you have to answer is, "What are you trying to go to?" And your answer is either really niching down and getting specific and specialized, or it's broadening out and expanding your offer.

So, niching down, if you are really good at graphics and you love to design websites, people will tell you, "Oh, you should start a web design company." And you'll think you should go and build websites all day long because that's what people want. Right? You have this gift to use and share.

For example, with niching down, you can get really narrow and you do logo design for only certain types of companies or a specific industry of clients where you've got a whole business where all you do is logo design. People come in and they're paying you five thousand, ten thousand, or fifty thousand dollars for logo design, and there are agencies like that—that exist because your whole specialization is one service, and there are huge margins, so you don't have to make a lot of logos to have a thriving business where you are not trading hours for dollars.

The other end of the spectrum is what you typically see, where you do logo design as a low-cost service. And you do media placement, and you do ad production, and you're writing ad copy and commercial scripts, you're filming it, you're doing all of that work that comes around it. Next, you're printing their logoed stationery, right? You've become all these other things that stack together with that offer. And that can work, if the key thing is that it's not you doing it all. You're finding somebody who does the logo design, another person who's doing the stationery and printing, and creating the media placements and all that for you as part of your business model.

In determining what the owner should focus on, how would you explain that process of identifying what you're good at, what you want to do, and what you should not be doing?

I'm a big believer that we all have these answers already, we just need to bring them forward to our awareness. So, what we do with a solopreneur or a small business owner that's looking to become a business seller but is stuck in the process of being a glorified freelancer, is the exercise I call "One hundred things."

I have them start writing down the things that they can do for a client. Anyone can do it, just start writing anything you're good at, a skill, a service, like graphic design, or creating a logo, put that down. Don't think too hard, just keep writing anything that comes to mind. Interestingly, most people start writing their list with the things that they don't like doing, actually. So, the first things on your list tend to be the things you'd pay *somebody else* to do, the stuff that you like the very least. I'll see things on the list like, "Oh, I'm good at taking these orders to the vendor for clients, so I'll put that down." Or "I'm good at taking client phone calls." So, the top of the list is all this stuff you can do but that you don't like doing. And then you get to the stuff that you actually enjoy doing, and that's the part that needs to be unpacked because I'll see people when they write their list of one hundred things, they'll initially be like, does it have to be one hundred? I'm sure that's a lot more than the things I can do. And they stall for a while when they write down the first ten, maybe twenty things.

But when they look at their list, they've written down things like "client proposals," right? Well, a client proposal, isn't one thing. Within creating a client proposal, you can unpack that to say: meeting with the client, listening to the client, interviewing and asking the right questions to the client, which is really a form of consulting. Then, they'll say: putting together a proposal, putting together the pricing, the steps in the process to deliver your service, which turns into defining your scope of work. And then you see that all of those things are different things you can do that should be spelled out in your list.

And the reason I get them to create this list of a hundred things is two-fold: One, you really need to value what you can do—clients get to a point where we can say, "You're doing all that. How much would the client have to pay to hire somebody to do all the things you can do?" And the client will say, "Well, you know, that job would be $20 an hour. And this job would be $50. But this job over here, that would be a few hundred dollars an hour. And when you add all that up, and they're getting that in one person, they quickly see that they're providing their client a very valuable service. And they also see that they should probably be charging a lot more for doing what they do.

The next part of what this exercise is doing is helping the client to see which pieces of what they can do are uniquely stuff they can do versus stuff that somebody else could do better. And this is what you were alluding to with my *Do, Delegate, or Eliminate Criteria*. If you own it, you should dedicate yourself to it. If it's something only you can do, like only you can do the live trainings. Only you can write your content the way you want it.

If you cannot delegate, can't eliminate, or can't automate the task, it's something you have to dedicate yourself, your time, and your energy to. Everything else gets put into one of those other buckets. The step I often like to include is asking the business owner to go through their day and say, "Which items do you like doing?" Because you really should be building a business that you like, and I would even say *love!* I need to throw that in because I believe very much that you should love what you're doing when you're spending most of your time doing it, do those things that bring you joy and ignite your passion, and really like, put you in flow, where you move into a place of optimal performance. Then, you're doing the best work you can do.

You can be one of the best in the world at it and time flies by. That's where you get that silly, oft-quoted adage that "if you're doing what you love, you're never going to work a day in your life." If you're spending the best chunks of your day, every day, doing things that are in your wheelhouse, you are performing optimally in your unique areas of strength.

Put down all of the things you can do, put down the things in that list that somebody else can do, and then put the ones that you want to do versus what you don't want to do. That might be as simple as saying, like, these are ones, these are twos and these are threes, where threes are items you're sure you don't want to do.

How do you move to working in just the skills that you have versus the skills that you love?

Start out with the baby steps of what do you most need to put in place next to remove yourself from the business. Start with what you can hand off or outsource. Sometimes it's more hours upfront to train and set somebody else up to take over that task, but in the long-term, it's going to give you back the time and, perhaps maybe even more importantly, the energy to do other things.

And that's a critical step because now you're taking an evaluation of how important the things you're doing are in relation to the outcomes you want to achieve.

I like to quantify a kind of scorecard for these things: there's stuff that you do that you can uniquely do. And when you do it, you're delivering at, let's say, a 10 or an 11 out of 10, right? You're amazing at it. You're delivering something that is top value and, if it has a value of 10 to your client, you might be stuck doing that thing, or you need to find somebody who does it as good as you.

Or better, right?

And that is pricey. That's one of those things where you have to evaluate the cost and trade-off. I've used this example before, that Home Depot has, inside of their corporate office, they have a catering service that brings in food for all of their employees. Home Depot could have owned that service, but instead they just found an existing provider of that service that does it better than them.

They bring those people in and it takes care of that for them, and they literally just pay money to somebody else to make that problem go away. As a business solution, we call it making your back of house business someone else's front of house.

If you find something that needs to be delivered to the client's expectation at your tier or higher, you need somebody to deliver at your level or higher.

At the other end of the example, if you do it at a 10 and somebody else may do that at a 6 or a 7, but the 6 or 7 on your scale is a client's ten, the client doesn't know any better or doesn't have the same expectations as you, then you're over-delivering on. It creates no additional value to the client, and one of the pieces I teach very heavily from my MBA background is this aspect of value creation, that profitability occurs when you create more value than you're collecting in cost to the client. That's the whole pricing game is to figure out how much this is worth to the client, and then you provide value that's greater than their cost. I always say, shoot for 10 times greater value just because it's a mental shift of

"I'm delivering what they asked for" to "I'm providing 10 times more than the cost I'm extracting from the client." That's a deal that the client will make all day long, come back with a glowing report, and share with other people. So, when I look at it that way, you want somebody who does it to the client's expectation, but exceeding that expectation with the overall delivery of your service, not each individual component, but the overall delivery of your service.

Back to my example that if you're doing video production, there's somebody else who's doing the casting, the camerawork, the scriptwriting, each of those pieces just needs to be at or above client expectation. The overall experience can be 10 times what the client's expecting by the way you deliver it, the way you package it, the customer service, the fulfillment, how much they feel taken care of. Those are the pieces that all play into it. And it's stepping enough out of it for you to say, "These are the things that somebody else can do as well or better than me," or "Somebody else *could* do instead of me, maybe at a lower quality, but without sacrificing, again, against the expectations of your clients."

The biggest obstacle is actually making that mindset shift and skill shift, and even that organizational shift, to ask, "What's the biggest obstacle to getting out of that day-to-day exchange of hours for dollars?"

How does a business owner make that shift?

Unfortunately, most business owners are Type A or High D personality who wants to have that kind of control over their business, but I think too often that personality type is what stops them from building a better business. Again, just because the person loves to cook starts a restaurant doesn't mean he needs to make this dish better than anybody else makes it. The egoist belief that I own the business means I have to be the one that makes this dish ensures your future as a glorified freelancer versus making the shift to ask questions as a business owner: how quickly and easily can I make this dish? how many times a day can I make this dish? How can I get more people to buy it and talk about? The answer to all of these questions comes back to: if I don't have to make the dish myself.

Your goal as a business owner is to create a process where you're delivering this product or service at or above the client expectations in the way that is most efficient and cost-effective way possible. That's simpler, right? Then, the obstacle really becomes defining what the result you're delivering is, understanding and establishing client expectations for it, which can only be done by talking to your customers, which goes to defining who your ideal customer is, and requires having the ability to detach your own ego, your own pride or sense of identity, from the result.

It comes from a self-definition. If you see yourself as a baker, you will need to spend a certain portion of your time baking to maintain your self-identity. Of course, if you want to be excellent at whatever you're trying to do, you'll have to put your time into doing that thing. If you're a graphic designer, you're going to spend your days graphic designing, and you can make a lot of money as a graphic designer, or, you know, as a baker, by being great at that thing.

The key to running a business and not just "doing the job" is to separate your identity from those things you do, and move into the entrepreneur mentality that your highest, most optimal value comes from creating a system where other people can do it.

The Ray Kroc example that people know from McDonald's is that he didn't set out to make the world's greatest hamburger. He set out to make a system where he could hire a teenager off the street that could walk in and deliver quickly, and cost effectively, a consistent product. So, that is a result-defined operation.

So, make that decision in your business, where you walk in and say, "What is the result our clients are expecting? How do we deliver that in the most cost-efficient and time-efficient manner?" And don't tie your own time and identity into delivering the work yourself. That's the fundamental difference between running a business and being a business owner.

www.ingramcontent.com/pod-product-compliance
Lightning Source LLC
Chambersburg PA
CBHW052319220526
45472CB00001B/181